The Fifth Amendment

Other titles in *The Constitution:*

The First Amendment
Freedom of Speech, Religion, and the Press
ISBN: 0-89490-897-9

The Second Amendment
The Right to Own Guns
ISBN:0-89490-925-8

The Fourth Amendment
Search and Seizure
ISBN: 0-89490-924-X

The Fifth Amendment
The Right to Remain Silent
ISBN: 0-89490-894-4

The Thirteenth Amendment
Ending Slavery
ISBN: 0-89490-923-1

The Fifteenth Amendment
African-American Men's Right to Vote
ISBN: 0-7660-1033-3

The Eighteenth and Twenty-First Amendments
Alcohol—Prohibition and Repeal
ISBN: 0-89490-926-6

The Nineteenth Amendment
Women's Right to Vote
ISBN: 0-89490-922-3

The Fifth Amendment

The Right to Remain Silent

The
Constitution

Harvey Fireside

Enslow Publishers, Inc.

40 Industrial Road   PO Box 38
Box 398   Aldershot
Berkeley Heights, NJ 07922   Hants GU12 6BP
USA   UK
http://www.enslow.com

To Douglas and Laura

Library of Congress Cataloging-in-Publication Data

Fireside, Harvey.
    The Fifth Amendment: the right to remain silent / Harvey Fireside.
      p. cm. — (The Constitution)
    Includes bibliographical references and index.
    Summary: An overview of the Fifth Amendment of the United States
Constitution, which defines and protects a citizen's rights
within the legal system.
    ISBN 0-89490-894-4
    1. Due process of law—United States—Juvenile literature.
2. United States. Constitution. 5th Amendment—History—Juvenile
literature. [1. Due process of law. 2. United States. Constitution.
5th Amendment—History.] I. Title. II. Series: Constitution (Springfield,
Union County, N.J.)
KF4765.Z9F57   1998
347.73'5—dc21   97-33476
                                     CIP
                                     AC
Printed in the United States of America

10 9 8 7 6 5

To Our Readers: We have done our best to make sure all Internet addresses in
this book were active and appropriate when we went to press. However, the author
and the publisher have no control over and assume no liability for the material
available on those Internet sites or on other Web sites they may link to. Any
comments or suggestions can be sent by e-mail to comments@enslow.com or to
the address on the back cover.

Photo Credits: Board of Regents, Gunston Hall Plantation, p. 33; Collection
of the New York Historical Society, p. 47; Courtesy of the State Museum of
Pennsylvania Historical and Museum Commission, p. 8; Courtesy of the
Virginia Historical Society, p. 44; Gregory Stapko, Collection of the Supreme
Court of the United States, p. 52; Harris and Ewing, Collection of the Supreme
Court of the United States, pp. 15, 87; Library of Congress, pp. 29, 43, 54, 63, 76,
78, 80, 83.

Cover Photo: NCRA

Contents

Introduction

Have you ever thought about the reason American government is unique? As a democracy, the United States provides for elections by the people. Yet there are foreign countries run by dictators that also hold elections. The working democracy in the United States is unique because it allows citizens to feel that the officials they elect really care about the views of the voters. The citizens are not afraid to criticize the government.

The Founding Fathers, those who wrote the Constitution, recognized the need to safeguard the rights of the people. After they wrote the Constitution in Philadelphia in 1787, they submitted it to conventions in the then-existing thirteen states for approval, or ratification. At many of these meetings, the delegates asked for a bill of rights to be added to it. James Madison, one of the leading delegates in Philadelphia, had at first opposed the idea. He thought such written guarantees would not really be effective. Later he yielded to the urging of Thomas Jefferson. As a member of the first Congress, Madison drafted the amendments that would become the Bill of Rights in 1791.

These first ten amendments to the Constitution can be seen as a special feature of our government. The First Amendment, for example, protects our freedoms of speech, of the press, and of religion. Neither Congress nor the state governments can take away these freedoms. The First Amendment gives us rights that we use every day, as we speak out, read our papers, or worship. But there are other parts of the Bill of Rights that are designed for emergencies. In this book, we will discuss the place of the Fifth Amendment. It assures our fair treatment by the police and courts if we are ever accused of a crime.

In the opening chapter, we see how the Fifth Amendment works. It prohibits double jeopardy (being tried twice for the same crime) and permits arrested people to remain silent and not testify against themselves in trials. The Fifth Amendment also contains a so-called Due Process Clause. It sets a basic standard of fairness in federal criminal and civil trials.

Perhaps the most powerful section of the Fifth Amendment is the one that states that anyone accused of a crime cannot be compelled to be a witness against himself or herself. This gives us the right to remain silent. The police must not make us confess to a crime by trickery or arm-twisting. The amendment also says that no one can "be deprived of life, liberty, or property without due process of law." The courts have had to interpret what due process means in individual cases. They have said, in general, that laws must be clear, specific, and applied fairly to all.

The second chapter explains the history of the Fifth Amendment. James Madison took most of his draft of the Bill of Rights from the state constitutions of that time. But the authors of these documents traced their ideas much farther back. These statements of the people's rights came from early English history. The kings, who had started out with total power, gave some legal rights to the nobles in the Magna Carta of 1215, the document that defines the rights of the citizens of England. Then, in the seventeenth century, the monarchs recognized the power of a government elected by the people. Rigged trials and forced confessions were abolished. This is how the fair standards for

This painting by John Froelich depicts the adoption of the U.S. Constitution at Independence Hall, Philadelphia, Sept. 17, 1787. George Washington, presiding, is standing at the right.

police and judges, eventually written into the Fifth Amendment, developed.

The third chapter bridges the gap between English and United States history. It shows how some of the Founding Fathers were, at first, not supportive of the idea of including a bill of rights in the Constitution. It then traces the change in James Madison's thinking—how he began as an opponent of the proposal, then became a supporter. But his original draft of seventeen amendments had to be reduced by Congress to twelve. Finally the state lawmakers adopted ten of these, and they are the Bill of Rights that we know today.

The actual form of each amendment, including the Fifth, owed a great deal to the men who crafted its language. The fourth chapter looks at the contributions of the following central figures: James Madison, Thomas Jefferson, George Washington, and George Mason. Mason had drafted the Virginia Declaration of Rights in 1776. He was the original author of several sections of the Fifth Amendment. The final draft, however, is credited to James Madison.

Yet the reason we have the Bill of Rights as part of our Constitution is not simply because a few brilliant men wrote it. It is also due to the people in many of the original thirteen states who did not want to accept the Constitution without it. In the fifth chapter we examine the battle for and against ratifying the Bill of Rights in the following key states: Pennsylvania, Massachusetts, Virginia, and New York. It became clear to the Federalists—the party favoring the Constitution—that it would not be accepted unless crucial amendments were added. The outcome in Virginia and New York was so close that James Madison realized he would have to follow the wishes of the people who were demanding the Bill of Rights. Many of them were Anti-Federalists who opposed the Constitution as setting up a central government that had too much power.

The sixth chapter presents the recent history of the Fifth Amendment. It was given its broadest interpretation by the Supreme Court under Chief Justice Earl Warren in the 1960s. The landmark 1966 case of *Miranda v. Arizona* provided police officers throughout the country with a warning they are required to read to suspects. The *Miranda* warning tells anyone accused of a crime that he or she has a right to remain silent; anything the suspect says can be used against the suspect at trial. This and other sections of the Fifth Amendment have been criticized as technicalities. In recent years, judges have become more easygoing in allowing certain incriminating statements to be used as evidence. Still, the use of *Miranda* warnings has not been shown to reduce the rate of criminal convictions.

The text of the Fifth Amendment is made up of only 109 words. Yet there are hundreds of important court cases that apply these words to the lives of the people. What the authors of the Bill of Rights said two hundred years ago needs to be adapted by judges and lawmakers to modern times and to a country that has grown beyond what was imagined long ago. The Founding Fathers, for example, never dreamed of telephones that could be tapped by police in order to gather evidence.

In this rather brief book you will not be able to find conclusive definitions of each term in the Fifth Amendment. But you will begin to see the outlines of the history that has brought the words of the text into our daily lives. And you may realize how important it is that the Constitution and the Bill of Rights limit the power of our government.

If you were ever in a neighborhood where a crime was committed, you could be questioned by the police. With several officers surrounding you, you might be so uncomfortable that you would be tempted to sign a confession just to get it over with.

At such a time, it would be a good thing to recall your rights under the Fifth Amendment. As a suspect, you should remember your right to remain silent and (under the Sixth Amendment) to talk to a lawyer.

This book is not really designed to be a self-help guide. But the history of the Fifth Amendment has a direct impact on each citizen. What the amendment means today was the outcome of many people who felt strongly about the need for laws that spelled out their rights. As you come to understand the Bill of Rights, you will appreciate that it does more than state abstract ideas. These ten amendments give us a feeling of security because they offer practical ways to be protected against injustice. By knowing and using your rights, you can make sure that they will continue to be available for use by all.

Your Rights Under the Fifth Amendment

What does the Fifth Amendment have to say about your basic rights? Imagine, for example, that you were stopped by a police officer outside your school and, without any warning, taken to jail. Since you were deprived of your liberty without proper legal steps, the Due Process Clause of the Fifth Amendment would have been violated. Now, what if the officer threatened to harm you unless you admitted having stolen something you did not steal? This would violate your right to remain silent. If there were a trial in which you were found guilty, the district attorney might try to bring new charges against you. If they applied to the same crime, that would violate your right to be protected from double jeopardy (being tried twice for the same crime).

In federal court and some state courts, if you had not been formally charged by a grand jury, bringing you to trial would also be a violation of the Fifth Amendment. Finally, imagine that some government official came to take over your front yard in order to widen your street. Here the amendment would let you protest the government's taking your property without just compensation, that is, without offering you a fair price for your land.

Each of these examples shows how the Fifth Amendment could affect your daily life. In each of these clashes with the law, one of your basic civil rights would have been violated. You and your attorney could go to court and have a judge protect your rights. The following five parts of this chapter will discuss how and when each section of the Fifth Amendment comes into play:

(1) The right to remain silent and not testify against yourself in court.

(2) The right against double jeopardy.

(3) The right to be formally charged by a grand jury.

(4) The right not to be deprived of life, liberty, or property without due process of law.

(5) The right to just compensation when the government takes your property.

The Right to Remain Silent

You have seen it often on television: The police are arresting a suspect. A police officer issues this warning: "You have the right to remain silent. Anything you say can and will be used against you." The police officer goes on to advise the suspect of the right to talk to a lawyer before being questioned. If the suspect cannot afford a lawyer, one will be provided if so desired.

This police routine has existed only since the Supreme Court decided the case of *Miranda* v. *Arizona*

The Justices of the 1966 Supreme Court are shown. They decided the case of Miranda v. Arizona. *From left to right: (sitting) Tom C. Clark, Hugo L. Black, Earl Warren, William O. Douglas, John Marshall Harlan, (standing) Byron R. White, William J. Brennan, Potter Stewart, and Abe Fortas.*

in 1966.[1] Ernesto Miranda was a twenty-three-year-old poor Hispanic American who had not finished the ninth grade. Though he insisted he was innocent when he came to trial, his confession to the police served to convict him of kidnapping and rape. Five of the nine Supreme Court Justices ordered him freed because the police had not told him of his constitutional rights—the right to remain silent under the Fifth Amendment and the right to have a lawyer under the Sixth Amendment.

If you stop to think about it, you may realize that it is not a bad idea to have the police make you aware of your rights if you are ever stopped by them. If you did not know that you do not have to answer questions, you might be so overwhelmed by police officers standing over you that you might blurt out something that would get you into trouble. The pressure would be even greater if the police took you back to the station house and put you into a locked room for questioning. Are you sure you could maintain your innocence after several hours of questions and threats?

Indeed, in such a room away from public view, the police might be tempted to use physical arm-twisting and even blows as part of the so-called third degree.[2] After all, they are trying to solve a crime. Instead of collecting evidence, which is tedious work, they might find it simpler to obtain a confession. After enough hours of such pressure, you might find it difficult to resist being persuaded to confess to something. Later, when you are facing a judge at a trial, it would be too late to argue that you did not really mean it when you confessed.

Before the *Miranda* decision, judges often took the word of the police officer who claimed a suspect's confession had been freely given. The public was generally too concerned about crime to be critical of the police.[3] People expected a suspect to be "cooperative" by doing and saying what police asked.

Where did this leave someone who believed he or she had been convicted of a crime in state court because of a coerced confession? The Fifth Amendment could not be used for relief. It applied only to federal, and not state, actions. There were no specific protections in the Fourteenth Amendment, either.

Fifth Amendment (adopted in 1791)

No person shall be held to answer for a capital, or otherwise infamous crime, unless on presentment or indictment of a Grand Jury, except in cases arising in the land or naval forces, or in the Militia, when in actual service in time of War or public danger; nor shall any person be subject for the same offense to be twice put in jeopardy of life or limb, nor shall be compelled in any criminal case to be a witness against himself, nor be deprived of life, liberty, or property, without due process of law; nor shall private property be taken for public use, without just compensation.

Fourteenth Amendment (adopted in 1868)

Section 1. All persons born or naturalized in the United States and subject to the jurisdiction thereof, are citizens of the United States and of the State wherein they reside. No State shall make or enforce any law which shall abridge the privileges or immunities of citizens of the United States; nor shall any State deprive any person of life, liberty, or property, without due process of law; nor deny to any person within its jurisdiction the equal protection of the laws.

Why did defendants in a criminal trial not turn to the Fifth Amendment instead of the Fourteenth? Because the Fifth Amendment is part of the Bill of Rights—the first ten amendments to the Constitution ratified in 1791. They were meant to protect citizens from actions of the federal (national) government. Most ordinary crimes are covered by laws of the fifty states. Until about sixty years ago, therefore, a defendant who claimed violation of his or her rights in a state court had to rely mainly on the Fourteenth Amendment. It covers actions by the states.

Then, in the mid-1930s, some Justices of the Supreme Court began to argue that key parts of the Bill of Rights should apply to the states as well as to the federal government. This argument became known as the incorporation doctrine.

The Right Against Double Jeopardy

The Justices of the Supreme Court disagreed on the specific articles of the Bill of Rights that were essential to "a scheme of ordered liberty" in states as well as federal citizenship. But in the next few years, the Supreme Court found that these basic rights included freedom of the press, speech, assembly, and religion (as stated in the First Amendment), as well as the right to counsel (an attorney) in a criminal trial (as stated in the Sixth Amendment).

A majority of the Supreme Court Justices agreed. Certain essential guarantees from the Bill of Rights should apply to the states through the Fourteenth Amendment. The Court did not support the defendant's plea that a prohibition of "double jeopardy" was among those rights, however.

Could a state prosecutor try you again if you were not convicted of a crime on the original charge? The answer is no. This is one of those rare instances in the history of the Supreme Court where it officially changed its mind. Thirty-two years after its original decision, a majority of the Justices held that protection from double jeopardy was one of those basic rights from the Bill of Rights.[4] It was "incorporated" in the Fourteenth. That means neither the federal nor the state courts can put you on trial twice on the same charge.

However, such rights as keeping silent and avoiding double jeopardy are not absolute. Even the right to free speech, from the First Amendment, does not mean, as Justice Oliver Wendell Holmes said, that you can falsely yell "Fire!" in a crowded theater.[5] Going back to the Fifth Amendment, how can a court force you to testify? If the court grants you immunity, that is, guarantees you freedom from prosecution for what you might say, then you must answer proper questions. Should you still refuse, the judge could charge you with contempt. You could be sent to jail until you do answer.

As for the protection against double jeopardy, you may be aware that occasionally defendants (such as O. J. Simpson) do undergo two trials. That may happen when there are separate criminal and civil charges. Criminal charges are brought by the state. Civil charges are filed by private persons who are trying to recover money for an injury. Both trials involve the same defendant and the same action. The degree of jeopardy or risk is different in each, however. In the criminal trial the defendant risks public punishment, for example, a prison term. In the civil trial, the defendant risks only paying damages to someone he or she has harmed.

The standards of proof also differ in criminal and civil trials. To be convicted of a crime you have to be found guilty beyond a reasonable doubt. In a civil case, however, the court can find you guilty by a "preponderance of the evidence." If more facts are presented against you than for you, you will be found guilty. Also, the jury in a criminal case needs to be unanimous—all twelve members must agree on the verdict. In a civil case there are generally fewer jurors than twelve, depending on state law. A two-thirds majority is usually enough for a decision.

There is another situation that looks like double jeopardy but is not. Both the federal and state governments can prosecute someone for the same crime. In 1991, for example, several Los Angeles police officers were accused of beating Rodney King, an African American. The officers were found not guilty of assault in a California state court. They were then charged under a Civil Rights Act in federal court of violating King's civil rights. This time the police officers were convicted.

The Supreme Court settled this issue of separate charges for the same crime in 1922, during the era of Prohibition, when making, possessing, and transporting liquor was illegal. Vito Lanza was a bootlegger who operated in the state of Washington. (A bootlegger was someone who illegally made and distributed liquor.) Lanza was convicted and fined for breaking the state's prohibition law. He was then prosecuted under the federal Volstead Act on the same evidence. (The Volstead Act was a law that provided a means to investigate and punish violators of prohibition.) The Supreme Court's unanimous decision in *United States v. Lanza* said the federal case could proceed.[6] This so-called Lanza doctrine still stands.

The Right to a Grand Jury Indictment

The opening section of the Fifth Amendment requires that anyone facing a criminal trial must first be indicted (formally charged with a crime) by a grand jury. A grand jury is a group of citizens who decide whether there is enough evidence of a crime to try a person in court. The only exception is made for personnel in the armed forces during a war or time of public danger. Does that mean that, if you are accused of robbing a candy store, your case will first be heard by such a grand jury? The answer is probably not. The requirement from the Fifth Amendment applies only to federal courts. States are free to use grand juries or some alternative pretrial procedure. Only about one third of the states still insist on grand juries in criminal cases.

A grand jury is a group of from twelve to twenty-three citizens who meet in secret to hear a prosecutor present evidence and witnesses against a defendant in a criminal case. Neither the defendant nor the attorney is present. A majority of these jury members is required to vote an indictment before the case can go to trial on a specific charge.

The most common alternative to a grand jury in state court is for the prosecutor to present evidence before a judge in what is known as a preliminary hearing. This hearing is public, with the defendant present, and the lawyer is able to cross-examine witnesses. The judge may then allow the prosecutor to file a document known as an information, roughly the equivalent of an indictment. If the evidence is not sufficient, the judge will order the defendant released.[7]

Both procedures, grand juries and preliminary hearings, are meant to protect you, if you have been accused of a crime, from an overenthusiastic prosecutor. It might seem to you that a grand jury would be a stronger check than a judge on such a prosecutor. You would probably prefer to have about twenty of your fellow citizens rather than just one decide whether the charges against you are valid or not. Yet in most big cities in the United States today, grand juries do not have the time or desire to be independent. In Illinois, for example, a grand jury hears about fifteen hundred cases in an average one-month term.[8] Jury members are, therefore, quite dependent on the prosecutor. As a rule they accept the recommendations made.

The Supreme Court was asked in 1884 to decide an appeal from Joseph Hurtado. He was a resident of Sacramento who was awaiting execution in a California prison. Hurtado had befriended José Antonio Estuardo, an immigrant from Chile. Then Hurtado learned that Estuardo was pursuing his wife. He assaulted Estuardo in a bar. While waiting to be tried, Hurtado shot and killed his wife's lover. Under California law, Hurtado's murder trial took place without a grand jury. It was based simply on a prosecutor's information. Hurtado was found guilty and sentenced to death.

Hurtado's lawyer argued that by trying a criminal defendant without a grand jury, the state had denied him due process. This is required by the Fifth Amendment, and should apply to the states under the Fourteenth Amendment. Justice Stanley Matthews spoke for a majority of the Court in *Hurtado* v. *California*. He found that the preliminary hearing satisfied the requirement for due process as long as it led to "a regular judicial trial."[9] Only Justice John Marshall Harlan dissented. He said that since a grand jury was required even before the country's founding, it must be included in the rights that the Fourteenth Amendment applied to the states. Yet it was the majority's view in *Hurtado* that made the grand jury an optional, not a required, step in state criminal trials. The grand jury clause of the Fifth Amendment, therefore, has remained one of the few provisions of the Bill of Rights that has not been incorporated, or required of the individual states.

The Right to Due Process

If you read the texts of the Fifth and Fourteenth Amendments presented earlier, you may have noticed a curious fact. Both amendments contain parallel guarantees of due process of law.

What is due process of law? The Supreme Court has offered two answers. The primary definition concerns the procedure followed by the government. So-called procedural due process protects you from arbitrary actions. This might include an official order against you that has not let you know specific charges or given you enough time to respond to them in a hearing. If the police or judge in a trial has not followed accepted procedure, you can appeal to have any action against you set aside. This is because that action did not result from due process.

Judges insist on proper procedures. They have also used the concept of substantive due process to protect individuals from state action. This is a more subjective concept than just checking on correct procedures.

President Franklin D. Roosevelt introduced all kinds of laws to regulate business during the opening days of his economic program called the New Deal. The Supreme Court at first found many of these laws were unconstitutional. By 1934, however, the Justices agreed with the president. Congress as well as certain state lawmakers also agreed that new regulations might be necessary during the period following the Great Depression. In a 5 to 4 decision, *Nebbia* v. *New York*, the Court agreed with New York State. It could set a minimum price for milk—at that time, nine cents per quart. New York's law limited the rights of businesspeople, but it was a reasonable (due process) way to improve the economy.

Leo Nebbia was a Rochester, New York, grocer. He

had been convicted for violating the state's Milk Control Act. According to Justice Owen Roberts, the conviction was unconstitutional. A state "may regulate a business in any of its aspects, including prices. . . ."[10] Further, "a state is free to adopt whatever economic policy may be deemed to promote public welfare." The dissenting opinion of Justice James C. McReynolds clung to the old theory of substantive due process. Here, the Justices struck down laws they believed to be unreasonable.

Nebbia marked the decline of so-called substantive due process. Judges could no longer second-guess lawmakers according to what they felt were basic rules of fairness. Judges could no longer go beyond a text in the Constitution or other law. They could not base a decision on what they thought the words implied. In the 1960s, the Supreme Court began to develop the right to privacy—due process in a new form.

In 1965, the Supreme Court set aside the conviction of Estelle Griswold for opening a birth control clinic for Planned Parenthood in New Haven, Connecticut. A state law of 1879 had prohibited the use of birth control, even by married couples. In *Griswold* v. *Connecticut*, Justice William O. Douglas spoke for seven of the nine Justices. They overturned the state law. Douglas found that people have a right to privacy. This was true even though such a right had not been spelled out in the Constitution.[11]

Justice Douglas found the right to privacy was implied by parts of the First, Third, Fourth, Fifth, and Ninth Amendments. Justice Hugo L. Black disagreed. He said he believed in the literal interpretation of the Constitution. According to him, it meant just what it said. New rights could not be invented by the Court. They could be added only by a constitutional amendment.

Yet the right to privacy has been expanded by the Supreme Court. It has been applied to protecting someone in a telephone booth whose conversation was picked up electronically by the FBI to convict him of illegal bookmaking.[12] In 1973, *Roe* v. *Wade* guaranteed a woman's limited right to an abortion.[13] The Court said that the state's invasion of a woman's right to privacy deprived her of liberty in violation of the due process clause. In 1990, the Court applied privacy and due process to the question of a right to die by a patient in a coma who was kept alive only by feeding tubes.[14] We can see how "due process" is far from a dry legalistic concept. It deals with crucial issues.

The Right to "Just Compensation"

Could you be affected by the final clause of the Fifth Amendment? It says, "Nor shall private property be taken for public use without just compensation." This is called the Takings Clause. It is based on the right of eminent domain. This is the power of government to take someone's property when necessary.

Suppose the town in which you live decided that it had to build a highway through what is now your living room. You might protest. Most likely, however, the highway department would prove that the road was necessary for the community. The only thing left for you or your lawyer to argue would be that the purchase offer was too low. Then it would be up to a court to decide what would be "just compensation."

In 1833, the Supreme Court decided that this Fifth Amendment clause was not applicable to the states.[15]

The Court saw things differently in the 1897 case of *Chicago, Burlington and Quincy Railroad* v. *Chicago*.[16]

The controversy arose from the city's expansion, due to the growth of industry. Chicago officials took over the lands of private citizens and railroad companies. They then offered what they considered just compensation. In a county court, the railroads were offered only one dollar for their property. Private owners received almost thirteen thousand dollars. The Illinois Supreme Court agreed that the county court had acted properly.

By a 7 to 1 decision, however, the United States Supreme Court found that the one dollar award for opening a street across a railroad track was not a fair award to the railroad. Indeed, it violated the Due Process Clause of the Fourteenth Amendment. From that time on, the Takings Clause has been incorporated into your rights against state action. Any unit of government—from the federal officials in Washington to the local ones in your town—must offer you just compensation when it takes over your property.

All rights are limited, however. There are cases where the government can simply seize property and give the owner nothing in return. If you owe taxes and cannot pay, the authorities might take your house or other valuables. Other laws enable the Drug Enforcement Agency to confiscate ships, planes, or other vehicles in which drugs were transported. The property of organized crime groups may also be seized under federal laws.

Ancestry of the Fifth Amendment

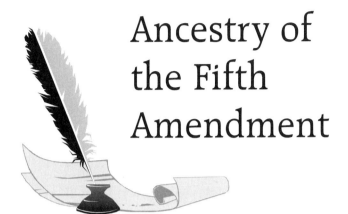

If you used the Fifth Amendment to protest an injustice, you could do so without fear. You could tell a police officer that you did not want to answer questions about a crime. You and the officer would both know that suspects have certain constitutional rights. But such protection for citizens is a fairly recent development in our history. In this chapter, we look at the important people in English and American history who made it possible for each of us to claim "the right to remain silent."

One of these courageous people was an English judge named Edward Coke. Although the king had Coke imprisoned in the Tower of London, Coke continued to fight for the rule of law. In 1628, Coke helped to have this idea included in the Petition of Right. Then, in 1638, a young man named John Lilburne withstood torture when he was accused of inciting rebellion against the king. His example helped establish the right against self-incrimination in English law.

The idea eventually caught on in the United States. In Pennsylvania, a printer named William Bradford refused to admit printing a certain document when questioned by authorities in 1692. His bravery impressed other colonists. When the new states declared their independence in 1776, they put the right to remain silent into law. In Virginia, George Mason wrote it into the Virginia Declaration of Rights. This marked the beginnings of the Fifth Amendment.

The Sections of the Fifth Amendment

There are five parts to the Fifth Amendment:

(1) The right to remain silent.

(2) The right against double jeopardy.

(3) The right to a grand jury indictment.

(4) The right to due process.

(5) The right to just compensation.

Each of these rights has centuries of legal history behind it. If you traced some of those central ideas, you would find their origins in the British colonies beginning in the early 1600s. The settlers who had come to America, however, brought with them ideas of law and individual rights that went farther back into the history of England. They expected to continue enjoying rights that their ancestors had won from the kings, starting in the thirteenth century. As Patrick Henry told the Virginia Assembly in 1765, they assumed from their charters "all the liberties, privileges, franchises and immunities that at any time have been held, enjoyed and possessed by the people of Great Britain."[1]

James Madison, depicted in this Chappel engraving, earned
the title of Father of the Bill of Rights for drafting the first
ten amendments to the Constitution.

"I'll Take the Fifth"

When you see someone on television say, "I'll take the Fifth," he or she probably has little awareness of the nearly eight hundred years of history that allow the use of that claim. When James Madison submitted his draft of the Bill of Rights to Congress in 1789, he had studied that history at length. Part of it was linked to documents in which the British Parliament had spelled out the people's rights. This set an example for the lawmakers in America. Part of it, however, makes up a story distinct from that of the American experience.

When the state lawmakers were unwilling to ratify the Constitution, they often commented on the absence of a bill of rights. They knew the British had adopted such a document in 1689. But what they generally lost sight of was that such British charters were written primarily to expand powers of the House of Commons. This is the directly elected part of Parliament. In this way, the powers of the king could be limited. In those early days, that meant that the rights of ordinary people were not especially protected. After all, Parliament was composed of elites: nobles, churchmen, and landowners.

Magna Carta and the Rule of Law

Still, there is a connection between the Bill of Rights in the United States and the Magna Carta (Great Charter) of Great Britain. For example, in its Chapter 39, the Magna Carta declares, "No man shall be captured or imprisoned or disseised [stripped of possessions] or outlawed or exiled or in any way destroyed . . . except by the lawful judgment of his peers and by the law of the land."[2] You may detect a parallel in this language to that of the Fifth Amendment. That part of the amendment states, "No person shall be . . . deprived of life, liberty, or property, without due process of law."

The Magna Carta's "law of the land" was indeed seen as the equivalent of "due process of law" by Edward Coke. He was a British judge and legal writer of the seventeenth century. Coke had been Chief Judge of the King's Bench. He was removed because he insisted that no man was above the law. In 1620, Coke was elected to the House of Commons. Here, he fought against the absolute rule of James I. The king had Coke imprisoned in the Tower of London for seven months.

Coke's Petition of Right

When Coke was released, he resumed the fight for due process of law with Charles I, who had succeeded to the throne in 1625. Coke was instrumental in getting the House of Commons to pass the Petition of Right in 1628. It stated "the supremacy of law." King Charles accepted this principle, though he continued to violate it in practice.[3]

The American colonists were familiar with Coke's achievements. They were determined to continue his tradition of laws that covered everyone. They also saw a turning point in British history. During the so-called Glorious Revolution of December 1688, James II, the last of the absolute Stuart rulers, was forced to flee the country. William and Mary would take the throne on February 12, 1689, but only if they agreed to conditions that became known as the Bill of Rights.

This English version was not at all the same as the later American listing of individual legal rights. They simply shared the same name. The British document was designed to put an end to the practice of monarchs like James II. He had suspended the laws when it suited him. The first eight amendments to the United States Constitution give specific guarantees to individual citizens. They are meant to protect citizens against actions by the government. Yet there is an overlap with the 1689 Bill of Rights. It also forbade "excessive bail, . . . excessive fines [and] cruel and unusual punishments."[4] The words are echoed in the 1789 amendments of James Madison.

Some scholars have argued that the true inheritance from Great Britain to American legal rights was not any written document. It was more the feeling that the colonists shared in the rights that people had won in the mother country. A formal statement of these rights had begun with the Virginia charter of 1606. The Massachusetts Bay charter of 1629 was followed in 1641 by the first detailed list of rights in the "Massachusetts Body of Liberties." It was copied in 1683 by New York and in 1701 by Pennsylvania. These forerunners of the Bill of Rights protected citizens from such things as double jeopardy in criminal trials and the taking of their property without just compensation.

George Mason's Virginia Declaration

A more recent influence on the amendments submitted by Madison was the Virginia Declaration of Rights. It had been attached to the constitution of that state when it declared its independence in 1776. Its author, George Mason, was the first person to put the old English right against self-incrimination into a written constitution.[5]

One of the commentators on George Mason's wording points out that he left out broader protections that had already become part of English and American law.[6] For example, the right to remain silent at that

A portrait of George Mason by Albert Rosenthal is shown here. Mason, author of the Virginia Declaration of Rights, was opposed to ratification of the federal Constitution.

time extended not just to the accused. It also applied to witnesses who might risk criminal penalties by their testimony. Further, the right covered cases in civil as well as criminal trials, even at a preliminary hearing. Mason's narrow clause makes it appear that only a criminal defendant can claim the right, and then only at the trial. Perhaps the reason for this is that Mason had never formally studied law, although he served as a justice of the peace in Fairfax County. Perhaps it is also due to the haste with which Mason wrote the declaration.

In any case, the Virginia Declaration of Rights became widely known in the other colonies. Most of the others used its language as a bill of rights in their new state constitutions. Two states during the so-called Glorious Revolution of December 1688—Connecticut and Rhode Island—kept their old colonial charters instead of writing new constitutions. Four others—New Jersey, New York, Georgia, and South Carolina—did not bother composing new bills of rights. They did not spell out a right to remain silent, but they did mention keeping the "common law" of England. That, at least, implied the right against self-incrimination, as well as the other protections that ended up in the Fifth Amendment.

English Common Law

There are various opinions on what makes up the common law. But the basic point that impressed the Founding Fathers was that it applied to the mixture of custom and judges' decisions that make up the British legal system. The rest of Europe followed law codes that had been established by the Romans. It took a revolution to make major changes in those codes. The common law, on the other hand, allowed for changes to develop gradually.

For example, in the Middle Ages (the period between ancient and modern times in western Europe) a good deal of English life was under the control of the Church courts. These Church courts decided how people were properly married or whether they had rights to inherited property. The courts also handled cases of ordinary crimes like murder.[7] If a bishop of the Church accused a layperson of a crime, he did not have to reveal the informant who had reported the crime. An accused person could not refuse to answer the charges without risking torture to make him or her confess.

King Henry II moved to limit the power of these Church courts. He may not have been concerned about protecting the rights of his subjects. More likely, the king needed money to build up his army. The Church had been profiting from the fines it imposed in its courts. It was forced to accept King Henry's constitutions in 1164. The enlargement of the king's courts meant a broader scope for judges who built up the common law.

The Jury System

What does this ancient history have to do with the American Bill of Rights?

(1) It meant that anyone accusing a person of a crime in England after 1164 had to do so publicly.

(2) It also meant that the accused person would be tried by twelve men chosen by the sheriff—a forerunner of the modern jury.

(3) It led, two years later, to an institution like the grand jury. These are the public accusers we inherited in the Fifth Amendment. Instead of private courts run by nobles, the medieval English kings required that accusations be made by sixteen men from the area.[8]

In its original form, the grand jury was designed mainly to enhance the king's power. It gave him a group of landowners in each county who reported any-one suspected of committing a crime. "Thus, the King had, in effect, created a citizens' police force as a means of ensuring central control over criminal pros-ecution."[9] The usual way of disposing of such cases was trial by ordeal. The accused person was subjected to severe pain or torture. It was believed that only the innocent would survive. For example, the accused might have a hand put into boiling water to see if an injury could be escaped. Or the accused could be thrown into a lake, to see if he or she escaped drown-ing without swimming. Not very many suspects were able to prove their innocence that way.

Jury Duty

You may know people who are not happy about serving on juries. It interferes with their work and earns them only token pay. Even long ago, the nobles of England also tried hard to escape jury duty. If the grand jury did not file enough accusations to please the king, the members would have to pay fines. The king relied on these juries to assess financial penalties that would keep money flowing to his treasury. Only by the late fourteenth century was the grand jury separated from the trial jury. It took until 1681, however, before the grand jury exercised an independent role in criminal trials. It could then begin to assume its modern function: protecting the accused from unfair, malicious, or political charges.[10]

Of course, the early English kings did not practice the rules that we consider essentially fair or part of due process. The regular courts allowed the common law to assure a public trial before a jury. There were also special trials behind closed doors, however. When a case involved questions of treason or religion, torture was used to extort confessions until the seventeenth century.

John Lilburne's Courage

These special courts were not abolished until 1641. The end of these courts led directly to the right to remain silent, which Madison included in the Fifth Amendment. The hero of the seventeenth-century story from England is a twenty-three-year-old Puritan named John Lilburne. He was accused in 1637 of having shipped seditious books (inciting rebellion) from Holland into England. Lilburne's formal education had ended when he was fifteen. His job was that of a clothier's apprentice. But he was also a stubborn, well-spoken man.[11]

The high officials of the Star Chamber (a court for treason cases) told Lilburne he must testify under oath. He refused, saying, "I am not willing to answer . . . any more of these questions because I see you go about this examination to ensnare me."[12] Lilburne underwent beatings and imprisonment. Until that time, those accused in the Star Chamber had to swear on the Bible they would answer all questions truthfully. This was the case, even though they had not been told the charges against them. If they refused, they could be imprisoned indefinitely for contempt of court. Other judges might still find them guilty of the original charge. Their silence might be taken as evidence of guilt.

Others like Lilburne faced an impossible choice. If they confessed, they could be executed for crimes against the Church of England. If they lied about their nonconformist religion, they believed they faced eternal damnation. When Lilburne was brought before the Star Chamber a second time, he again refused to swear the required oath. He was found guilty of contempt and sentenced to a fine of five hundred pounds, whipping, punishment in the pillory (a wooden frame with holes for the head and the hands), and another stretch in prison until he would testify. The huge fine would have meant that the government seized all of Lilburne's possessions. "I was condemned," he later wrote, "because I would not accuse myself."[13]

The courage of Lilburne is shown by his endurance in the face of his punishment on April 16, 1638. He was tied to the back of a cart for the two-mile walk from prison to the pillory. Every few steps he was whipped with knotted cords, more than two hundred times. When he was put into the pillory, with holes for his head and arms, he addressed a large crowd that had gathered. Despite his pain, he spoke eloquently about his resistance to the forced oath. It went against both the 1628 Petition of Right and "the law of God; for that law requires no man to accuse himself."[14] The incredible performance of Lilburne made him a national figure.

The reign of King Charles I ended in civil war. The victorious Puritans came to power. They were determined to free the victims of the king's oppression.[15] Their leader was Oliver Cromwell. He made his first speech to the new government on behalf of releasing John Lilburne from prison on November 9, 1640. A few days later, Lilburne and other Puritan prisoners were indeed set free.

The government then investigated the two courts that had routinely used torture to obtain forced confessions. It was finally agreed that these courts should be done away with. On July 5, 1641, the king reluctantly signed the bill. It was a victory for the common law. The act said that from then on, all trials were to be held "in the ordinary Courts of Justice and by the ordinary course of the law."[16] From that day on, it was forbidden to force any "of the King's subjects . . . to accuse themselves by or upon their own oaths in any criminal case whatsoever."[17]

American colonists were generally proud to claim their rights from English common law. Yet at certain times and places, the colonists allowed these rights to lapse. In Massachusetts, for example, torture had been outlawed in 1641, as it had been in England. But in 1692, the town of Salem held the notorious witchcraft trials. There the judges used torture against some of the women who had begun by declaring their innocence.[18] In the end, about fifty of the women confessed to being witches. If they had not, they might have joined the nineteen others who were hanged because of "evidence" from the spirit world.

William Bradford's Example

In Pennsylvania colony, at about the same time, there was a power struggle between John Blackwell, a Puritan who was deputy governor, and the Quakers in the council. One of the council members had paid William Bradford, a printer, to publish copies of the colony's charter. It was to be used in the campaign against Blackwell. The deputy governor summoned Bradford before the council in 1692. He was charged with not having obtained the necessary license.

Bradford stood his ground, however. He used his right to remain silent under the common law. Blackwell asked him, "I desire to know from you, whether you did print the charter or not, and who set you to work."[19]

Bradford answered, "Governor, it surely is an impracticable thing for any man to accuse himself, thou knowst it very well." Blackwell threatened, "Well, I shall not much press you to it, but if you were so ingenuous [frank] as to confess, it should go the better with you." Bradford answered, "Governor, I desire to know my accusers, I think it very hard to be put upon accusing myself." Blackwell said, "Can you deny that you printed it: I know you did print it and by whose direction, and will prove it, and make you smart for it too since you are so stubborn."[20]

Blackwell had quite a lot of power in the absence of the governor, William Penn. But the printer stuck to his right against self-incrimination. Soon Blackwell was forced to resign.

It turned out to be the spirit of the printer Bradford rather than that of the deputy governor Blackwell that shaped colonial law. The tortures and forced confessions at Salem, Massachusetts, became only a footnote in that legal history.

The colonists looked up to persons accused who stood their ground. One of them was John Peter Zenger. He was a printer whose newspaper attacked the royal governor of New York. In 1735, a grand jury twice refused to indict Zenger on a charge of seditious libel. The printer was finally tried on the prosecutor's information. (This is an alternative to the grand jury.) He was acquitted. Zenger's trial was "the germ of American freedom—the morning star of that liberty which subsequently revolutionized America."[21]

The independent spirit of those accused helped shape the language of the Fifth Amendment. Many courageous people, English and American, staked out the protections of individuals from the government. This led to the five sections of the Fifth Amendment. The history of this struggle was well known to the authors of the Bill of Rights. It is evident in their speeches and writings.

How the Fifth Amendment Was Born

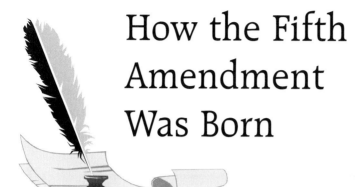

Whether or not you enjoy certain rights today under the Fifth Amendment is spelled out basically by the courts. They interpret the laws based on their understanding of the Constitution. However, the authors of the original document set aside plans for a bill of rights. The first ten amendments to the Constitution had to wait to be added by Congress and the states in 1791. In this chapter we look at the reason for this delay. Much of the story centers on James Madison and his opposition to the Bill of Rights.

The delegates to the Constitutional Convention assembled in Philadelphia from May to September 1787. They were there to try to strengthen the newly formed United States. They debated long and hard about how to shape the new national government. How would the power of the large states be balanced against that of the smaller ones? Would the rights of property holders be safe against the majority of voters? Was the presidency such a powerful office that it could lead to dictatorship? What rights were the original states giving up to the new federal government?

Compromises in Philadelphia

The delegates argued furiously. Eventually they settled on a number of compromises. The House of Representatives would be based on the population of each state. In the Senate each state—large or small— would have two senators. These solutions were worked out under the guidance of George Washington. He was the president of the convention and had commanded the army that won the Revolutionary War. The debates and the text were carefully recorded by another Virginia delegate, James Madison.[1] Madison's notes were not allowed to be published until after his death. The discussions in Philadelphia were kept secret. In this way, all the delegates would take common responsibility for the proposed Constitution.

Like many of the other Founding Fathers, Washington and Madison were wealthy landowners. They were concerned with setting up a strong and stable system of government. They felt an urgent need to replace the Articles of Confederation. This set of laws had kept the states in a loose union since they declared their independence from Great Britain in 1776. Now, something better was needed. While they were hammering out the Constitution, the delegates were not too concerned with how the people would be protected from the new government.

Was a Bill of Rights Needed?

On August 20, 1787, Charles Pinckney of South Carolina proposed that some guarantees of legal rights be added to the Constitution. He wanted trial by jury to be assured in civil as well as in criminal trials.

This drawing by Allyn Cox shows some of the leading delegates to the Constitutional Convention who met in Benjamin Franklin's garden. Left to right: Alexander Hamilton, James Wilson, James Madison, and Franklin.

Pinckney's proposal was referred to the Committee on Detail, which had to approve language before it was included in the draft Constitution. No one voted for it.[2]

On September 12, just five days before the convention adopted the final text, two other delegates spoke about how the document badly needed a bill of rights. Elbridge Gerry of Massachusetts joined with George Mason of Virginia to propose such a statement of basic legal rights. Their proposal was rejected by a vote of 10 to 0.

On September 15, Edmund Randolph of Virginia said that he was worried about the "dangerous power given by the Constitution to Congress."[3] He suggested that a second meeting was necessary. Mason agreed that a second convention at a later date would help to "know more of the sense of the people." Not a single vote was cast, however, in favor of Randolph's motion for a second meeting.[4]

Roger Sherman of Connecticut argued that the constitutions of most of the states already had a declaration of rights. These guarantees were not affected by the new federal Constitution, said Sherman, "and being in force are sufficient."[5]

A portrait of Edmund Randolph by an unknown artist is shown here. Randolph, from Virginia, worried that the Constitution placed too much power in the hands of Congress. He favored holding a second meeting to resolve the disputes brought up by the Constitutional Convention.

Sherman's argument did not satisfy Gerry, Mason, and Randolph. They refused to sign the final Constitution. (Only thirty-nine of the fifty-five delegates did sign.) All three wanted a second convention to be held before adopting a final document. Madison was among the majority of delegates who supported the Constitution as it had been written at Philadelphia. Together with Alexander Hamilton of New York, Madison became a leader of this group known as Federalists. They were opposed by the Anti-Federalists in a two-year struggle that took place state by state on whether or not to adopt the new Constitution.

Making a New Government

What became known as the Constitutional Convention had been called together on February 21, 1787, by the Congress. It had been meant for "the sole and express purpose of revising the Articles of Confederation" and bringing back suggestions to Congress and the state lawmakers. It took something like a revolution for the delegates to disregard their instructions, draft a plan for an entirely new government, and submit it to special meetings of the voters in each state.[6] Madison became one of the inner circle of six or so delegates who created this revolution. They scrapped the old system, in which the state governments really ran the Congress. It was something like the way in which delegations from different countries operate the United Nations today.

In place of the Continental Congress, they set up three branches of a new government: executive, legislative, and judicial. The key proposal, introduced by Randolph and Madison, was known as the Virginia Plan. It shifted the power that had been given to the separate states to the central government. The House of Representatives would be the one branch elected directly by the voters. The only unit that would still give states a voice was the Senate. State lawmakers, under the original plan, would nominate senators. They, in turn, would be elected by the House. Both houses together would then choose a president, limited to one term, and a council of national judges.

The shape and powers of these branches were greatly changed as a result of the debates at the convention. What remained, however, was the insistence of Madison and his allies on a strong central government. It had the power to make laws that would control the actions of states and individual citizens. Jefferson had asked Madison to study republics from ancient Greece to modern Switzerland. Madison had done his homework well. He showed this by quoting the history of governments in his speeches at Philadelphia and, later, in his essays urging voters to ratify the Constitution.

The Federalist Papers

Madison, Hamilton, and their junior partner, John Jay, collaborated on a series of letters that were later published in a book known as *The Federalist Papers*. There are eighty-five letters in all. They were published under the pseudonym (pen name) of Publius in New York City newspapers beginning on October 27, 1787. They were meant to influence the voters to approve the Constitution. This was especially true in New York State, where Governor George Clinton was openly opposed to it. If this state voted no, it would probably spell defeat for the Constitution. New York, Pennsylvania, and Virginia made up about half the entire country's population.

This portrait by Ezra Ames shows George Clinton, first governor of New York. Clinton opposed ratification of the Constitution.

Madison is credited with writing twenty-six of *The Federalist Papers*. He also coauthored three more of them with Hamilton.[7] They contain forceful arguments for the Constitution. Debaters in the various states could use these arguments to put people's minds at ease. One of the most famous, "Number Ten," addresses fears that under the new government various "factions" (today called interest groups) would fight violently. Madison said that group struggle was inevitable. A large country such as the new United States, however, would have a great many groups. In the new Union it would be much harder for any one group, such as poor farmers, to take control.[8]

It was left to Hamilton in *The Federalist Papers* to explain the absence of a bill of rights in the Constitution. In "Number Eighty-Four," he wrote that some states like New York had no bill of rights in their constitutions either. Yet the people were protected by maintaining the rights they had enjoyed under "the common and statute law of Great Britain."[9] The original Bill of Rights in 1688 was forced upon the king by Parliament, Hamilton said. The new Constitution of the United States, however, put the people in charge, so that "bills of rights . . . are unnecessary"; indeed, they might even "be dangerous."[10] If you spelled out "liberty of the press," for example, it might give somebody the wrong idea that the press could be restricted. It was better just to leave such rights understood and to rely "on the general spirit of the people and of the government."[11]

Hamilton's arguments did not persuade the large number of people who were concerned about the absence of a bill of rights. After all, most of the states had followed Virginia's "Declaration of Rights" in 1776. They put specific protections into their constitutions. The Anti-Federalists were now painting the dangers of the new federal government. Who could be sure that the new, more powerful national government would not oppress the people? How could it hurt to make sure by spelling out the people's rights?[12]

Massachusetts Votes Yes, But . . .

The specific debates in some of the key states will be described in Chapter 5. Here we are focusing on the origins of the Bill of Rights. That leads us to the state convention, which met in Massachusetts to consider ratifying the Constitution on February 7, 1788. It overcame the objections of the Anti-Federalists by tying its approval to a set of informal amendments. In the words of John Hancock, the convention's president and the first signer of the Declaration of Independence, such changes "would remove the fears and quiet the apprehensions of many of the good people of this Commonwealth and more effectually guard against an undue administration of the Federal Government."[13]

In other words, Massachusetts approved the Constitution but with doubts. It wanted to make sure that the new national government would not be too powerful. For example, it wanted to limit the federal power to "lay direct taxes." (Under the existing Articles of Confederation, Congress had to ask states to make contributions.) In its list of nine amendments, Massachusetts also sketched two provisions of a future bill of rights: providing a jury trial in civil cases and requiring a grand jury indictment for criminal trials. Finally, the state urged its future representatives in Congress "to exert all their influence and use all reasonable and legal methods" to have all nine amendments adopted.[14]

The Struggle in Virginia

Massachusetts had shown the Federalists that they might have to make a deal with their opponents to secure ratification of the Constitution. This pattern of "gentlemen's agreements" was repeated in Virginia, New York, and North Carolina. The Virginia struggle was one of the fiercest. The Anti-Federalist group there was led by Patrick Henry. He was the five-term governor who became famous for his words, "Give me liberty or give me death!" The only way the Federalists were able finally to win a close 89 to 79 vote of approval for the Constitution was to agree to consider twenty amendments that would make up "a declaration or bill of rights."[15]

Several of the amendments that eventually ended up in the Bill of Rights can be traced to these Virginia proposals. For example, the Fifth Amendment's right against self-incrimination comes from one of Virginia's provisions. In what later became the Due Process Clause of the Fifth Amendment, Virginia proposed (in clumsier language), "That no freeman ought to be taken, imprisoned, or seized of his freehold, liberties, privileges, or franchises, or outlawed, or exiled, or in any manner destroyed or deprived of his life, liberty, or property, but by the law of the land."[16]

What concerned James Madison was not the statement of such legal rights. He was worried about an additional twenty amendments proposed at the Virginia convention by the Anti-Federalists. These included the requirement for states to agree each time the national Congress wanted to "lay direct taxes or excises."[17] Another provision limited the power of the national government to have a "standing army . . . in time of peace." This would have to be approved by a two-thirds vote in Congress. The same two-thirds vote would be required for "any law regulating commerce."[18]

Such drastic changes in the proposed Constitution would require a second national convention. All the delicate compromises at Philadelphia—between large and small states, for example—would have to be negotiated all over again. It was, therefore, a happy surprise to the Federalists when Virginia governor Edmund Randolph argued for adoption of the Constitution without another convention. The final vote gave them a slim victory. They would not have to pay the price of a second convention, however. They just had to agree informally to consider the forty proposed amendments at a later date.[19]

The Close Vote in New York

The Federalists in New York fought the same kind of battle as had taken place in Virginia. This time, fifty-five amendments were proposed. Some urged adoption of the Bill of Rights. Others seriously weakened the powers of the national government.

Hamilton and Jay led the fight for adoption of the Constitution at the state convention in Poughkeepsie, New York. Melancton Smith spoke for the Anti-Federalists. He criticized the Constitution as "a beast dreadful and terrible and strong exceedingly, having great iron teeth—which devours, breaks in pieces, and stamps the residue with his feet."[20]

It looked like a deadlock between the two forces. Then John Jay outmaneuvered the critics of the Constitution. He drafted a letter to Governor Clinton. The letter indicated his group's willingness to have a bill of rights added by amendment. Smith, however, did not want to give up his demand for a second national convention.[21] The vote on July 23, 1788, was 31–29 in favor of the Constitution.

A Lesson for the Federalists

Eventually, twelve states approved the Constitution in their conventions. According to Article VII of the draft, it would go into effect when nine states had ratified it. New York made number ten. Soon the only holdouts were Rhode Island and North Carolina. The Anti-Federalists in Rhode Island managed to defeat ratification in a freeholder election. North Carolina had a tie vote, 184 to 184, at its first convention in August 1788. This was not enough to secure adoption. A second convention in November 1789 won North Carolina's approval, by a 168 to 136 majority.[22] The close votes in two of the major states—New York and Virginia—drove home a lesson to the Federalists. They needed to rally greater popular support to their cause.

John Jay, one of the authors of The Federalist Papers, who helped secure ratification of the Constitution in New York is shown here.

Madison Changes His Mind

Madison realized that it was preferable to support a bill of rights than to have the whole governmental structure unravel. His mentor, Thomas Jefferson, had told him in a 1787 letter from Paris that the draft of the Constitution appeared workable. Jefferson had, however, insisted that "a bill of rights is what the people are entitled to against every government on earth, general or particular; and what no just government should refuse, or rest on inference."[23] The following year, Jefferson had specified such basic rights as liberty, trial by jury, *habeas corpus* (a court order to have a jailed person brought into court to verify the lawfulness of his or her detention), the absence of economic monopolies (in which large companies take over), and freedom of the press and religion.[24]

In his reply to Jefferson on October 17, 1788, Madison changed his mind. At first, he thought a bill of rights was unnecessary because the Constitution itself protected the people by setting up the rule of law. Then, he saw how strongly the Anti-Federalists had felt about the absence of a bill of rights. He was ready to support it as a set of amendments to the Constitution.[25]

The critics of the Constitution were able to block the election of Madison as a senator from Virginia. These critics controlled the state lawmaking bodies. When Madison decided to run for the House of Representatives, the Anti-Federalists named James Monroe to oppose him. Madison's new position on adding "essential rights" to the Constitution helped him defeat Monroe.[26]

True to his word, on June 8, 1789, Madison introduced seventeen amendments to the first session of

Thomas Jefferson, as painted by Charles Wilson Peale, is shown here. Jefferson, while an envoy to France in 1787, wrote James Madison to urge adding a bill of rights to the Constitution.

Congress. Most of them were taken from the Virginia Declaration of Rights. At least two, however, had not been included in any state constitution. They were that no person could be forced to give up private property without just compensation (the future Takings Clause of the Fifth Amendment); and that no state could infringe on the rights of conscience, freedom of the press, or trial by jury in a criminal case (omitted from the Bill of Rights).

Madison's original motion was submitted to the Select Committee in the House for review. This committee had a member from each state. Madison was the Virginia delegate. He had asked that the list of citizens' rights be inserted directly into the Constitution. Most of them would go in Article 1, Section 9, in the list of congressional powers. The committee was chaired by Roger Sherman of Connecticut. It decided that the future Bill of Rights belonged at the end of the document. "We might as well endeavor to mix brass, iron and clay," said Sherman, "as to incorporate such heterogeneous articles."[27]

Madison shepherded the amendments through Congress (as described in Chapter 4). Then they were submitted to the states. New Jersey and Maryland were the first to accept them, early in 1790. North Carolina, which had not yet ratified the Constitution, passed both that document and the twelve amendments. Clearly, the addition of the Bill of Rights had helped achieve the Federalist victory.[28] Five of the states defeated two of the proposed amendments: changing the method by which members would be elected to the House of Representatives, and making Congress wait one session before members could give themselves a pay raise. But the remaining ten amendments were adopted by the required three fourths of the state lawmakers on December 15, 1791. That is accepted as the birthday of our Bill of Rights.

By that time there were fourteen states in the United States. It took eleven of them to adopt amendments. The final state to do so was Virginia. Three states—Massachusetts, Connecticut, and Georgia—had not ratified. They waited until the one hundred fiftieth anniversary of congressional adoption of the Bill of Rights, in 1939, to make it unanimous.

Fathers of the Fifth Amendment

In the second chapter, we saw that the Fifth Amendment has a long history. In a sense, the reason that you can refuse to answer questions by the police is that this right was tested for centuries. It goes all the way back to people who stood up to the king's power long ago in England.

There is, however, a more direct link to the actual language of the amendments that became the Bill of Rights. The men known as the Founding Fathers took great pains with each word they added to the Constitution. At first, they expected to rush the document through adoption by the states. Then, when they realized what a close battle it would be, they became willing to consider adding a list of the people's rights.

In this chapter, we look at the part played in this process by James Madison, Thomas Jefferson, George Washington, and George Mason. Mason had been the author of the Virginia Declaration of Rights. It contained clauses that were used later in the Fifth

Amendment. Mason opposed ratification of the Constitution, mainly because it lacked a bill of rights.

James Madison and the Bill of Rights

The person who is usually given the credit for adoption of the Bill of Rights, including the Fifth Amendment, is James Madison. He was also the fourth president of the United States. During the early days of his political career, however, he was one of our most brilliant Founding Fathers. He had a major hand in shaping the document that became the Constitution of the United States.

Before the Philadelphia convention, Madison had not been a nationally known figure. He had achieved a reputation in Virginia. He was an able member of the convention that in 1776 declared the state's independence. But his star really rose when he joined the council that advised the governor. It was through that post that he worked closely with Thomas Jefferson. Though Jefferson was eight years older than Madison, he became his lifelong political guide and friend.

Jefferson was a brilliant thinker, writer, architect, educator, and farmer. He excelled in many fields. He had grand visions, such as the equality of all men that underlay the Declaration of Independence he composed in 1776. Jefferson's mansion, called Monticello, is one of the most popular national tourist attractions. Madison was a much more private man than Jefferson, yet he, too, was a genius. He constructed the arguments to fashion the political system of the new nation. He had the persistence to push these plans through committees and councils. He also had the ingenuity to put together the compromises that made the ideas a reality.

Madison graduated from the College of New

Jersey, now called Princeton University, in 1772. Two years later, he joined his father in the Committee of Safety. This was the country's voice of protest against British rule. In 1779, the Virginia Assembly chose Madison as one of the state's five delegates to the Continental Congress. He was elected for a four-year term. He analyzed the weakness of the congress in letters to friend Thomas Jefferson.

In 1780, Madison returned home until he was elected as a state lawmaker to the General Assembly. Here he worked behind the scenes to get passed Jefferson's bill guaranteeing religious freedom. (Jefferson had been sent to Paris as American minister to France.) Madison was shy, short, and not a great speaker, but he became known as a scholar.[1] Jefferson shipped him from Paris two trunks full of books on history and politics. Madison seemed to have read them all. He always had the facts and ideas to back up any proposal.

When he joined the fifty-five men who would draft a new Constitution, Madison, age thirty-six, was among the youngest. His influence, however, was soon so great that historians have called him the father of the Constitution. For one thing, he had prepared for his assignment in Philadelphia during the preceding winter and spring by writing an essay. "Vices of the Political System of the United States" gave an insider's view of what had been wrong with government under the Articles of Confederation. It concluded that the existing loose system was too weak to be patched up.

In 1787, there were no tape recorders or stenographers to capture the exact words of a debate. The main source we have of the convention that drew up the Constitution is Madison's notes. They give an extensive record of the various proposals offered by the delegates.[2] Madison's accounts of the proceedings are still consulted by the Supreme Court when it tries to analyze the "original intent" of clauses in the Constitution. These notes show that major differences were resolved through compromise.

Madison had helped shape the Virginia Plan. It also won the support of other large states, such as New York, Pennsylvania, and Massachusetts. Madison also saw value in the proposal of the smaller states, known as the New Jersey Plan. Finally, he backed the Connecticut compromise. This resolved the issue by giving each state two senators. Its representatives were determined by population. Madison was also key in designing the system of "checks and balances." This would assure that the federal government could not be dominated by any one of its branches: legislative, executive, or judicial.

Madison seemed to turn a deaf ear to several of the delegates who wanted a bill of rights to be a central part of the Constitution, however. Madison thought that the "checks and balances would be worth far more than 'parchment barriers' to restrain arbitrary power. He disliked absolute prohibitions that would have to yield to political necessity. He relied finally on enlightened public opinion under a system of popular government."[3]

In other words, Madison was not especially concerned that the new government would turn into a dictatorship. The institutions—House, Senate, president, courts—were designed to restrain one another. A list of citizens' rights was not necessary. It could even hurt the government. Any single right, such as habeas corpus (the need to justify someone's imprisonment), might have to be limited in an emergency like a rebellion. The real safeguard of people's rights was their active involvement, through elections, in the government.

Even Jefferson, Madison's good friend, could not persuade him that the Constitution would be improved by a bill of rights. It should be noted, however, that Jefferson's list of rights that he specifically wanted added in July 1787 to the Constitution left out those that were finally included in the Fifth Amendment, such as the right to remain silent.[4]

Madison wrote to Jefferson in October 1788. He was not convinced that the absence of a bill of rights was a shortcoming of the Constitution. By that time, it had become evident from debates at the various state conventions that many people strongly disagreed with Madison on that issue. Yet Madison was still only lukewarm about adding a list of rights as amendments that "might be of use."[5]

He assured Jefferson that people were adequately protected by "the limited powers of the federal Government." Further paper guarantees might only blind people to the fact proved by history. Their rights could be "violated . . . by overbearing majorities in every state." Madison wrote to Jefferson on October 24, 1787.[6] In his letter, Madison reported that Richard Henry Lee, a prominent Virginian in Congress, had endorsed the idea of adding amendments to the Constitution. Lee was trying to counter George Mason's objections. The Philadelphia delegates were looking for a way to convince all the states to accept the document.

Here Madison was preparing a strategic retreat from his earlier opposition to a bill of rights. He was trying to prevent a barrage of amendments that would weaken the national government. If additions to the Constitution would help secure its adoption in the key states of Massachusetts, New York, and Virginia, he would rather take charge of the process himself. Madison's position had shifted to support for a limited number of amendments. He thought this should persuade people that the new federal government would not intrude on their basic rights.

In a letter to George Washington on September 30, 1787, Madison reported the proposal of Richard Henry Lee. "It was contended that Congress had an undoubted right to insert amendments, and that it was their duty to make use of it in a case where the essential guards of liberty had been omitted."[7]

Madison came only reluctantly to the support of the Bill of Rights. Some historians think he could have saved everyone a lot of trouble if he had listened to the critics at the Philadelphia convention—chiefly, Elbridge Gerry of Massachusetts, and George Mason and Edmund Randolph of Virginia. They urged that basic rights be included in the Constitution.[8] Others point out the masterful way in which Madison used the promise to add amendments later. It was crucial in winning approval of the Constitution in some of the key states. Keeping the Bill of Rights as a bargaining chip allowed Madison to deflect the Anti-Federalists from their main object. They could no longer attack the added powers of the new central government over the states.[9]

The rights spelled out in the Fifth Amendment were not included in the original document first proposed in September 1787. It took another two years, until September 1789, before Madison's version received the approval of the House and Senate. Ratification by three fourths of the states was completed on December 15, 1791. Only then did the first ten amendments become part of the Constitution.

This portrait of James Madison was done by Charles Wilson Peale. Madison, while a congressman, drafted the amendments that became the Bill of Rights.

Madison intended to carry out the promise he had made to the voters of Virginia who had elected him to Congress. He had to get George Washington's agreement, however, to amend the Constitution so soon after its ratification. As a close adviser to the first president, Madison could slip the suggestion into his first inaugural address. On April 30, 1789, Washington first urged caution before making "alterations" in the new government. Then he suggested acting on the Bill of Rights.[10]

Washington wrote Madison in May 1789. Washington was not very enthusiastic about the amendments. They seemed, however, to be something the people would welcome. Said Washington,

> I see nothing exceptionable in the proposed amendments. Some of them, in my opinion, are importantly necessary, others, though in themselves (in my conception) not very essential, are necessary to quiet the fears of some respectable characters and well meaning men. Upon the whole, therefore, not foreseeing any evil consequences that can result from their adoption, they have my wishes for a favourable reception in both houses.[11]

In this way, Washington added his prestige to the proposed Bill of Rights that Jefferson had endorsed. Madison could now move it through Congress. The country's leader was saying that he approved the amendments not because they were really essential. Washington saw adoption of the Bill of Rights as an effective tactic. It would broaden support for the new government, without giving up any essentials of the Constitution.

George Mason and the Fifth Amendment

We should give credit not only to Madison, Jefferson, and Washington, but also to the critics who had argued that the Constitution was unacceptable without the Bill of Rights. The most deserving of this group to be considered a father of the Fifth Amendment is George Mason. He was another Virginia landowner who took a leading role in the independence movement in 1776. He was also an important part of the formation of a new government afterward.

Unlike Washington, Jefferson, and Madison, Mason had no taste for public life. His neighbors had to persuade him to be a delegate to the state's and then the country's conventions. Mason was a lifelong sufferer from a painful disease called gout. He would beg to be excused as soon as possible, to return to his beloved mansion, Gunston Hall. It was not far from Washington's home in Mount Vernon.

Mason's participation in the Virginia Convention of May 1776 was perhaps his finest hour.[12] On May 27, only nine days after Mason's arrival, the committee presented a declaration. It had been largely written by Mason in his room at the Raleigh Tavern. On June 12, the delegates unanimously adopted the Declaration of Rights.[13] In Chapter 3, we saw that one article of the declaration—the eighth of sixteen—contained two aspects of the Fifth Amendment: the right to remain silent and the Due Process Clause.

Mason deserves credit as the author of that statement in 1776. Yet Madison clearly expanded it in 1788. He added the right against double jeopardy, the right to a grand jury, and the right to just compensation. He also phrased the other two rights in clearer and more direct language than Mason's. For example, Madison substituted due process for Mason's law of the land. He drew upon not just the Virginia Declaration of Rights. He also used the lists in other state constitutions and the amendments proposed by seven of the state ratifying conventions.

It seems that the Fifth Amendment in its final form reflects the careful craftsmanship of Madison. It had taken him a long time to change his mind. But when Madison dropped his opposition to the Bill of Rights, he echoed the tactical argument offered by Washington in his May 1789 letter. On June 8, Madison told the House of Representatives how Congress could convert wavering critics of the Constitution by amending it.[14]

There were still many citizens, he said, who felt they had fought the Revolutionary War in vain. These critics of the Constitution had to be won over. The Federalists could do this by giving the people the amendments they desired, as long as they did not undermine the new government.

Madison acknowledged that doubts remained about the absence of a bill of rights. Even two years after the Philadelphia convention first met, a number of people were still concerned that their government might repress them. Madison suggested that amendments be scattered throughout the text, to quiet those fears. His Federalist friends were prepared to be generous about granting these rights. Then they could unite the country behind the new government.

Indeed, Madison proved to be more than generous. He put all his efforts behind the tedious work of drafting and moving the amendments through the committees in Congress. He agreed to having the Bill of Rights follow the text of the Constitution. He had previously wanted it scattered throughout the text itself. Finally, he tried to put extra force behind it. It would have to apply to the states as well as the federal government.

Madison proposed such an amendment saying "no state shall violate the equal rights of conscience, or the freedom of the press, or the trial by jury in criminal cases."[15] If that so-called lost amendment had passed, it would have saved more than 140 years in our history before key parts of the Bill of Rights were applied by the Supreme Court to the states under the incorporation doctrine. (That doctrine is explained in Chapter 1.)

In any case, that important addition was among the amendments of Madison that were adopted by the House of Representatives on August 24, 1788. In a closed session, the Senate then whittled away some of the language, including the lost amendment. Madison's original seventeen amendments were rearranged into twelve by the Senate.

On September 9, the Senate version was returned to the House. Here it was reargued. Finally, a conference committee of the two chambers met to work out the final text. Madison was one of three House members on that committee. It also included three Senate members. Madison was able to persuade the others to keep some of his original language. This is most noticeable in the First Amendment's clause on religious liberty.[16]

On September 23, Madison gave the conference report to the House. The report was accepted the next day, by a vote of 37 to 14. On September 25, the Senate added its vote of approval. The Bill of Rights was finally ratified by three fourths of the states on December 15, 1791. It then became an essential part of the Constitution, and fulfilled the promise that Madison had made on June 8, 1789.

The Fifth Amendment and the other parts of the Bill of Rights owe their origins to many sources. But the chief author remains Madison. He put it all together and pushed it through the committees and conferences in Congress until it was enacted into law. He understood that it would answer the demands of the people and bring them closer to the goals of their new government.

The Battle for Ratification

To whom do you really owe the rights you enjoy under the Fifth Amendment? Whom do you have to thank for the limits on government power, such as the right to remain silent if you are accused of a crime? In Chapter 4, the credit seemed to go to the Founding Fathers led by James Madison. In Chapter 2, a longer look back into English history focused on courageous figures like Edward Coke and John Lilburne. Here, we will look at many lesser-known figures. These are the Anti-Federalists who argued against adopting the Constitution without the Bill of Rights.

In state after state, from 1787 to 1789, these Anti-Federalists said that the people's basic rights had to be spelled out. The Federalists also said that the people's basic rights had to be spelled out. The Federalists realized this two-year struggle would be close. They might win approval of the Constitution in the required nine states, but unless all the big states signed, that might be a hollow victory. What would the United States be without Pennsylvania, Massachusetts, Virginia, and

New York? We will look at the fight for and against ratification in those key states. That will show how amendments suggested by the Anti-Federalists found their way into the Bill of Rights.

Amendments From the Opposition

James Madison emerges as the central author and mover of the Fifth Amendment. He took up the cause of the Bill of Rights only in response to opponents of the Constitution, however. His main source for items to offer as amendments was a pamphlet. It compiled the more than two hundred suggested additions offered by seven of the state ratifying conventions. The Federalists had secured adoption of the Constitution in those states by promising to consider amendments as soon as possible.

There were two kinds of amendments: the ones that would weaken powers of the central government such as control of a national army and of interstate commerce by the Congress, and the ones that would protect citizens from the government. These ended up in the Bill of Rights. Madison and his colleagues were trying to avoid the first kind at all costs. It threatened to undo their painstaking work at Philadelphia. They came to realize that the second kind could be accepted without any real risk.

In this chapter, we focus on the struggle to ratify the Constitution, in 1787 and 1788. It had been a brainstorm of the Philadelphia delegates not to expect all states to adopt the document before it went into force. This was a nearly hopeless task. The approval of just nine states would suffice "for the establishment of this Constitution. . . .[1] Yet it was also clear that the new system would not really work unless all the major states signed on. The small states were generally eager to ratify the Constitution. It gave them the same two senators as the large states. This also meant two extra votes in the electoral college that would choose the president. Delaware was the first state to ratify. It gave unanimous approval to the Constitution.

It may not be apparent from standard American history texts just how close the struggle was in some of the key states. The Anti-Federalists offered terrible predictions of the dictatorship that would be exercised by the new Congress. It would have an array of powers far exceeding that of the old Continental Congress, and by the newly created office of president.[2] The Federalists admitted that their new government would be an experiment. They assured the people, however, that they could trust the leaders—including Benjamin Franklin, George Washington, and James Madison—who had drawn up the Constitution. Also there was no going back to the Articles of Confederation. Thirteen separate armies, tax systems, and sets of laws were simply not acceptable. Under that old system, no joint action was possible unless all of the states agreed unanimously.

The Anti-Federalists argued that until a bill of rights was added either by a second convention or a series of amendments, they could not support the Constitution.

The Battle in Pennsylvania

The first major test of the respective strength of the two forces—for and against ratifying the Constitution—began in Pennsylvania. This was the state that hosted the convention. Only a day after the delegates had adjourned on September 17, 1787, the new Constitution was read. On September 29, the state lawmakers set November 6 as the date to elect delegates to a ratification convention. That meeting was to take place on November 20.

The debate in the state's press had actually begun in August. This is when rumors held that the Philadelphia convention was drafting a new Constitution rather than patching up the Articles of Confederation. The state's politics had been dominated by two political parties since 1776. One Pennsylvania party was known as the Constitutionalists. It was supported by farmers, and it had been behind the state constitution. The other state party, known as Republicans, combining farmers, tradespeople and professionals, opposed it.

When it came to the new federal Constitution, they reversed roles: the Republicans were for it. The Constitutionalists were against it.[3] Some historians contend that ordinary farmers may have looked to state governments to postpone payments of their debts. Large farmers and merchants expected a new national government to promote trade and foster economic growth.[4] In the winter of 1787, Shays' Rebellion in western Massachusetts had united debt-ridden farmers. They joined in an uprising that frightened establishment figures throughout the states. The uprising gave a big push to leaders who wanted a strong national government. Other historians believe the supporters and opponents of the Constitution were divided not so much by economic interest as by age.[5] The younger voters generally were open to this novel "experiment." Older ones were generally against it.

Before events got under way in Pennsylvania, the Anti-Federalists realized that the pro-Constitution forces were seizing the upper hand. They decided to boycott the session scheduled for September 29. Their absence would block a quorum. That is the number of assemblymen needed to conduct business. An angry crowd carried two of the Anti-Federalists against their will to the assembly. This created a quorum that set the election date for the state convention.[6]

The Anti-Federalists now tried to win a majority opposed to the Constitution. If they could not achieve that goal, they would call for a second convention. Such a new session might undo the original document and turn back the clock to the loose government of the Articles of Confederation.[7] Their scheme collapsed when the Federalists won twice as many seats, forty-six to the Anti-Federalists' twenty-three. Their leaders were three of the men who had been delegates to the Philadelphia convention: Robert Morris, James Clymer, and James Wilson.

On November 26, Wilson countered the critics' call to add a Bill of Rights before the document could be taken up. There was no need to spell out such specific rights, said Wilson. "To every suggestion concerning a bill of rights, the citizens of the United States may always say, 'We reserve the right to do what we please.'"[8] In other words, the framers of the Constitution had always meant to reserve all the rights not assigned to the federal government to the people. By spelling out a select few rights, the delegates would be unduly restricting the power left to the people.

The Anti-Federalists realized the hopelessness of their cause in Pennsylvania. They sent a delegate to discuss strategy with Richard Henry Lee, of Virginia. He had just met with Elbridge Gerry, of Massachusetts, and Governor George Clinton, of New York. They all agreed that the best hope to rally the opposition forces was to have states postpone action until April or May 1788. Then they could unite behind a series of amendments or insist on calling a second constitutional convention. The motion to delay Pennsylvania's action until the following spring, "so that the deliberate sense of the people could be obtained," was defeated, however.[9]

The delegates ratified the Constitution, 46 to 23, on December 12, 1787. Pennsylvania became the second state to do so after Delaware. The Federalists had beaten back amendments, but the Anti-Federalists had a good argument in a losing cause. Twenty-one of them signed an article explaining their disagreements on December 18. It spelled out fourteen amendments that they had failed to get adopted. One of them contains the beginning of what would become the Fifth Amendment. The Anti-Federalists demanded the right to remain silent when charged with a crime and the right not to be imprisoned except by a jury trial.[10]

The Anti-Federalist statements were distributed by the Pennsylvania delegates to those in other states. They would be used in the next round of debates. A major battle was looming at the Massachusetts convention. It had opened in Boston on January 9, 1788. The momentum was on the side of the Federalists. New Jersey and Connecticut had just given lopsided victories to their cause. Connecticut's convention came just before that of Massachusetts, from January 3 to 9, 1788. The Federalists overwhelmed their opponents 128 to 40.

The Outcome in Massachusetts

James Madison was aware that the result in Massachusetts would influence its neighbors, New Hampshire and New York. He wrote Edmund Randolph on January 20, 1788, "The decision in Massachusetts, in either way, will decide the voice of [New York]."[11] The Federalists were aware that a strong opposition had been forming in Massachusetts since Elbridge Gerry had launched the first attacks on the Constitution in October 1787.[12] The Anti-Federalists seemed to have the lead among convention delegates. Samuel Adams, one of the grand old revolutionary leaders, found the Constitution undemocratic.

Adams was said to have the allegiance of the tradesmen of Boston. However, on January 7, 1788, three hundred eighty of these merchants showed up at a rally in the Green Dragon Tavern to make their support of the Constitution known. The convention opened the next day. Amos Singletery called for a bill of rights. He was answered by Joseph B. Varnum. He claimed it was not necessary because Congress was limited in writing to specific powers. The rights granted by the Massachusetts constitution would, therefore, not be affected.[13] Abraham Holmes said there was nothing to stop Congress from compelling those accused of a crime to testify. Individual officials, unchecked by a grand jury, could arrest anyone they pleased.

The debate for and against a bill of rights contin-ued until the presiding officer, Governor John Hancock, worked out a compromise. Hancock was a very popular figure who had his eye on becoming the country's vice-president. He agreed to push for ratifi-cation. First, he would have a committee recommend amendments to be passed by the initial session of Congress. On February 4, nine such amendments were moved. Number six had a link to the future Fifth Amendment. It proposed "that no person shall be tried for any crime, by which he may incur an infa-mous punishment or loss of life, until he be first indicted by a grand jury."[14]

John Hancock, pictured here, is famous for being the first signer of the Declaration of Independence. Hancock presided over the Massachusetts state convention that ratified the Constitution that he favored.

Hancock's action brought many of the delegates, including Samuel Adams, to the Federalist side. The position of Adams had begun to shift when he heard of the pro-Constitution views of the Boston merchants. This was especially true of the shipbuilders who were among his close longtime friends.[15] The final vote, on February 6, 1788, was a narrow victory for ratification, 187 to 168. The Federalists had managed to win here only by agreeing to accept amendments. This pattern was to be followed in other states, like Virginia and New York, where the outcome was still in doubt. Conventions in those states also echoed the concerns heard at length in Boston. There was a need to propose a bill of rights in the future.

The Struggle in Virginia

The Virginia delegates assembled to take up the new Constitution on June 2, 1788. By this time, eight states had already ratified it. If Virginia would join them, the new government would go into force. George Washington had written,

> The plot thickens fast. A few short weeks will determine the political fate of America for the present generation and probably produce no small influence on the happiness of society through a long succession of ages to come.[16]

We know that Washington, Madison, and Jefferson were Federalists—supporters of the new Constitution—from Virginia. But they were opposed by an illustrious group of Anti-Federalists. This group was led by the former governor and brilliant speaker, Patrick Henry. As mentioned earlier, he is known for his famous 1775 speech, "Give me liberty or give me death." It led to a break in America's relations with Great Britain. Now Henry spoke often and at length

Patrick Henry, a fiery orator and former governor of Virginia, led the Anti-Federalist forces in the state against ratification of the Constitution.

against ratifying the Constitution. He felt it would destroy authority of the individual states on which the people's liberty was based. He gave eighteen speeches on the twenty-three days of the convention. One speech lasted for seven hours. "I see great jeopardy in this new government," said Henry. "I see none from our present one, the Confederation, which has carried us through a long and dangerous war."[17] Without amendments to limit its powers, the Constitution was "the most fatal plan that could possibly be conceived to enslave a free people."[18]

George Mason was an old friend of Patrick Henry's. Their friendship went back to the early pre-Revolutionary days in 1765. They had both opposed the British tax on tea. Mason was one of the "fathers" of the Fifth Amendment. He was also the author of Virginia's Declaration of Rights in 1776. Yet he had refused to sign the Constitution in Philadelphia. He saw it as a threat to the freedom of the American people.[19] Madison had written about Mason at the state's ratifying convention in June 1788. "He is growing every day more bitter and outrageous in his effort to carry his point, and in all probability, in the end, will be thrown by the violence of his passions into the politics of Mr. Henry."[20]

Virginians had to face the fact that they would either be part of the new government or left out of it. As Edmund Randolph said in his concluding speech, "The accession of eight states reduced our deliberations to the single question of Union or no Union."[21] Randolph had been converted from an opponent of the Constitution to a key supporter.

It came down to the choice of amending the Constitution either before its ratification—as Henry and Mason wanted—or afterward. On June 25, Henry's proposal to make amendments, including a bill of rights, a condition of ratification was defeated 85 to 88. The Federalists were willing to accept a recommendation for amendments after ratification. That motion passed, 89 to 79. Among the twenty proposed amendments, ten eventually made it to the Bill of Rights.[22]

New York's Crucial Vote

The next key decision was up to New York. There seemed to be an anti-Constitution majority among that state's voters. As Alexander Hamilton wrote to James Madison on July 2, 1788, Federalist speeches had persuaded only a few of the doubters. "Our arguments confound, but do not convince."[23] Hamilton commanded the Federalist forces against the Anti-Federalists.

Historians suggest that it was not really Hamilton's speeches that converted the opponents. Hamilton knew his forces were outnumbered. He fell back on threats. If the state did not ratify the Constitution, New York City would secede.[24] But that only alienated the Anti-Federalists, whom John Jay, a coauthor of the *Federalist Papers* with Hamilton and Madison, had to calm.

SUPPLEMENT

TO THE

Independent Journal,

New-York, July 2, 1788.

In our Independent Journal of this Morning, we announced the Ratification of the New Constitution by the Convention of Virginia: For the gratification of our Readers, we publish the following particulars, received by this day's post:—

Ratification of the New Constitution, by the Convention of Virginia, on Wednesday last, by a Majority of 10:—88 for it, 78 against it.

WE the delegates of the people of Virginia, duly elected, in pursuance of a recommendation of the General Assembly, and now met in Convention, having fully and fairly investigated and discussed the proceedings of the Federal Convention, and being prepared as well as the most mature deliberation will enable us to decide thereon, DO, in the name and on behalf of the people of Virginia, declare and make known, that the powers granted under the Constitution being derived from the people of the United States, may be resumed by them whensoever the same shall be perverted to their injury or oppression, and that every power not granted thereby, remains with them, and at their will: That therefore no right, of any denomination, can be cancelled, abridged, restrained or modified by the Congress, by the Senate, or House of Representatives, acting in any capacity, by the President, or any department or officer of the United States, except in those instances where power is given by the Constitution for those purposes: That among other essential rights, the liberty of conscience, and of the press, cannot be cancelled, abridged, restrained or modified by any authority of the United States.

With these impressions, with a solemn appeal to the searcher of hearts for the purity of our intentions, and under the conviction, that whatsoever imperfections may exist in the Constitution, ought rather to be examined in the mode prescribed therein, than to bring the UNION into danger by a delay, with a hope of obtaining amendments previous to the ratification:

We the said delegates, in the name and in behalf of the people of Virginia, do by these presents assent to and ratify the Constitution, recommended on the 17th day of September, 1787, by the Federal Convention, for the government of the United States; hereby announcing to all those whom it may concern, that the said Constitution is binding upon the said people, according to an authentic copy hereto annexed, in the words following:—

[*Here followed a copy of the Constitution.*]

A letter from Richmond advises, " that a motion for previous amendments was rejected by a majority of EIGHT; but that some days would be passed in considering subsequent amendments, and these, it appeared, from the temper of the Convention, would be RECOMMENDED."

NEW-YORK: Printed by J. and A. M'LEAN, FRANKLIN'S HEAD, No. 41, Hanover-Square.

The Independent Journal *of July 2, 1788, announced Virginia's ratification of the Constitution by a ten-vote margin. The news persuaded New York delegates to follow suit a month later.*

New York governor George Clinton, a critic of the Constitution, chaired the convention. Melancton Smith was the floor leader of the Anti-Federalists. He assumed a key role. Smith had been a pioneer Revolutionary, a sheriff, and a judge. He was also involved in land speculation. He was a delegate to the Congress under the Confederation. He had been a loyal follower of Governor Clinton. Smith moderated his opposition to the Constitution as news arrived that two more states had ratified: New Hampshire on June 21 and Virginia on June 25. With ten states forming the new government, New York would have to fall in line.[25]

Before he gave up the fight, Smith proposed a series of amendments that amounted to a bill of rights. The Federalists were willing to go along with Smith's motion. They would not, however, accept his condition that the amendments would be submitted to a second constitutional convention. Still, Smith's acceptance of the Constitution—even though only if conditioned on amendments—split the Federalist majority on July 17 and 18.

Hamilton had renewed hope that New York would ratify if it accepted Smith's deal. But Madison told him on July 20 that a compromise was not possible if conditional ratification was necessary. The Constitution should not be subject to the opponents' "right to withdraw [approval] if amendments be not decided on . . . within a certain time."[26] Madison insisted that "the Constitution requires an adoption [as a whole] and *for ever*." Subsequent amendments, such as a bill of rights, might be possible, but "that is not the material point at present."[27]

John Lansing was a strict Anti-Federalist. He rejected the compromise unless it spelled out New

York's conditional ratification—saying yes to the Constitution only if it contained a bill of rights. On July 23, Smith moved to replace Lansing's conditions with an informal understanding. His motion was to ratify in confidence that amendments would be added later by Congress. It passed with a narrow majority. On July 26, the delegates approved the Constitution and a lengthy set of amendments. The vote of 30 to 27 was very close.[28] Smith's action did not sit well with his political supporters. They denied him the chance to be a United States senator. This, in effect, ended his political career.

The amendments suggested by New York set a record for length. They included a total of fifty-seven proposed changes. Many of them were taken from Virginia's list. The right against self-incrimination, for example, was found in Virginia's Declaration of Rights. New York delegates—Federalist and Anti-Federalist alike—wanted it added to the Constitution. The final wording of that clause, "No person . . . shall be compelled to be a witness against himself," was due entirely to Madison, however. Another future section of the Fifth Amendment—the Due Process Clause—owes its wording to the New York proposal.

Other States Fall in Line

After New York acted, North Carolina was the major holdout. It initially rejected the Constitution by a tie vote 184 to 184 on August 4, 1788. The Bill of Rights that Congress had passed and submitted to the states now won over some of the undecided delegates. At a second convention, from November 16 to 23, 1789, North Carolina ratified by a vote of 136 to 168.

It took more than two years, from the time Congress approved twelve of Madison's amendments

This portrait of Alexander Hamilton was painted by Charles Wilson Peale. Hamilton, was one of the authors of The Federalist Papers, and a key figure in securing the adoption of the Constitution in New York.

in September 1789 until ten of them had been ratified by the required three fourths of the states in December 1791. Some of the state delegates thought the amendments were too weak. In Virginia, the forces of Patrick Henry felt Madison had betrayed them by not moving their whole long list of proposed changes.

The ten amendments that would eventually become the Bill of Rights were passed in the meantime by New Jersey, Maryland, North and South Carolina, New Hampshire, and Delaware. New York ratified on February 24, 1790. Governor Clinton, however, thought the amendments were too "trivial and equivocal [flawed]."[29] Pennsylvania, Rhode Island, and Vermont also ratified. That left Virginia to resolve its deadlock. Finally, this key state became the eleventh to adopt the Bill of Rights on December 15, 1791. That made this document an official part of the Constitution. This was the first time in history that these rights of the people had been spelled out as the basic law.

The Fifth Amendment Today

In the first chapter, you became familiar with your rights under the Fifth Amendment. The next chapters described the history of these rights, from medieval England to colonial America. Chapter 5 explained how the language of the amendment was developed. Yet you still may not be able to tell exactly how this applies to you. For example, can you start claiming your right to remain silent when you are first questioned by police or only when they actually arrest you? Can you do this at your home? What about at the police station? Does this rule apply to minors?

The general wording of the Fifth Amendment does not contain many specific explanations. Therefore, since its passage in 1791, the amendment has had to be interpreted by the courts. The Supreme Court has spelled out your rights in hundreds of cases. It gave the broadest meaning to the right to remain silent in the *Miranda* decision of 1966. The following year, the Justices extended this right to young people tried in juvenile court.

Since *Miranda*, the Justices appear to have had second thoughts. They have allowed certain types of confessions to be used in a trial even without the *Miranda* warning. But the warning is still generally required by law. This chapter reviews these basic changes in the Court's thinking. It also touches on recent conflict about the meaning of the Takings Clause. This deals with your right to have "just compensation" for property taken by the government. This right has been questioned by agencies protecting the environment. The Justices have had to find a balance between the rights of property owners and those of the government.

Current Concerns

Current controversy about the Fifth Amendment often centers on whether some of its provisions—such as the right to remain silent—are being interpreted too loosely. Are court rulings making the job of the police more difficult?

The Miranda Decision

The 1966 Supreme Court opinion in *Miranda* v. *Arizona* was a landmark decision. It set the standard of fairness for police questioning of a suspect under the Fifth Amendment. As Chief Justice Earl Warren said for the majority, "Prior to any questioning, the person must be warned that he has a right to remain silent, that any statement he does make may be used as evidence against him, and that he has a right to the presence of an attorney."[1]

Justice Warren explained the need for such a rule by quoting a report by the Commission on Civil Rights in 1961. It stated that "some policemen still resort to physical force to obtain confessions." Indeed,

Warren said, "Only recently in Kings County [Brooklyn], New York, the police brutally beat, kicked and placed lighted cigarette butts on the back of a potential witness under interrogation for the purpose of securing a statement incriminating a third party."[2] Even more widespread than physical violence, Warren said, was psychological pressure on suspects in an isolated room. Sometimes this was achieved through the use of trickery. He quoted from police manuals that told investigators to pretend sympathy for a suspect or to minimize the seriousness of the offense. These methods were said to be helpful in obtaining a confession.

Warren read the entire sixty-one-page opinion to a packed courtroom on June 13, 1966. A law professor later called it "the most famous, and most bitterly criticized, confession case in the nation's history."[3] Justice Warren had taken more than an hour to read the *Miranda* decision on behalf of five of the Justices. Then the four dissenting Justices had their turn. Justice John Marshall Harlan, "his face flushed and his voice occasionally faltering with emotion," denounced the decision. He termed the majority opinion "dangerous experimentation" at a time of "a high crime rate that is a matter of growing concern."[4] This "new doctrine," Harlan

Chief Justice Earl Warren wrote the Supreme Court opinion in Miranda v. Arizona *in 1966.*

claimed, would tip the "balance in favor of the accused."

The two sides on the Supreme Court disagreed not only on the future effects of the decision. They also differed on whether narrow or broad definitions should be used when defining "custody" or "interrogation." During the remaining years of Chief Justice Warren's tenure, the Court spelled out its views on this issue in only one other case.

In the 1969 decision of *Orozco* v. *Texas*, Justice Hugo Black spoke for the majority in extending *Miranda* rights to suspects questioned at home.[5] Texas officials had argued that since a murder suspect was "interrogated on his own bed, in familiar surroundings, our Miranda holding should not apply," said Black. They were wrong to limit the right to remain silent to questioning at a police station. The Court had "declared that the warnings were required when a person being interrogated was in custody at the station *or otherwise deprived of his freedom of action in any significant way.*"[6]

The Warren Court was attacked by Richard Nixon in the 1968 presidential campaign for being "soft on criminals." Messages to "Impeach Earl Warren" appeared across the country. Warren later admitted that the "attack centered on the case of *Miranda* v. *Arizona.*"[7] Yet Warren claimed, there

> was really nothing new in this except to require police and prosecutors to advise the poor, the ignorant, and the unwary of a basic constitutional right in a manner which had been followed by the Federal Bureau of Investigation procedures for many years. It was of no assistance to hardened underworld types because they already knew what their rights are and demand them.[8]

Limiting Miranda Rights

Warren Burger was named Chief Justice by President
Nixon in 1969. Then the Court majority shifted to a
narrow reading of the Fifth Amendment. For example,
a 1976 decision allowed the informal questioning of a
man at home by Internal Revenue Service (IRS) agents
without the *Miranda* warning. It led to criminal
charges of tax fraud.[9] In 1977, the Court let stand the
self-incriminating testimony of a parolee who showed
up voluntarily at a police station.[10] In a 1980 decision,
a majority of Justices adopted a narrow view of
"interrogation," where *Miranda* would apply.[11] Two
policemen were taking a suspect in for questioning.
They said that a shotgun missing in a murder would
be dangerous if found by a child. The fact that the
suspect then pointed out where the weapon was
hidden was voluntary, according to the Court. It was
not judged to be the product of interrogation.

William H. Rehnquist became Chief Justice in
1986. The Court continued to chip away at *Miranda*
rights of suspects.[12] A mentally ill man told the police
that the "voice of God" told him to confess to a murder.[13] The Court's majority in 1986 said that was not a
violation of the Fifth Amendment. Police in 1988 were
also not required to read *Miranda* warnings to drivers
whom they questioned at traffic stops.[14]

In short, *Miranda* has not been overruled. The
Court has limited the circumstances where confessions are considered illegal, however. One expert sees
the Justices taking a more narrow view of the Bill of
Rights since the Warren Court.[15] The Court once
focused on protecting an individual's constitutional
rights. It is now balancing society's needs against
those individual rights.[16] Currently, the Justices are
giving the benefit of the doubt to the police about the

free nature of a confession. This holds true as long as there is no proof that the confession was obtained by force.

Miranda's *Effects on Crime*

Has the use of *Miranda* warnings really hampered police work? There were certainly attacks on the *Miranda* decision "by police, prosecutors, politicians, and media" from the day it was announced.[17] President Nixon called it "a victory of the 'crime forces' over the 'peace forces.'"[18] Three decades later, it "remains a symbol of controversy in American society and continues to be assailed by its many critics."

Indeed, in the 1980s under President Reagan, the Department of Justice urged the Supreme Court to overrule *Miranda* altogether. A noted law professor finds that the procedure set by *Miranda* has had generally good effects. "*Miranda's* enduring impact has been to increase the level of professionalism during the investigative stage of the criminal process."[19] Police officers now act with greater fairness. Most of the time they obtain testimony anyway. Suspects with criminal records are much more likely to assert their "right to remain silent." Most suspects, however, waive (give up) this right and talk to the police.

Do lawyers later succeed in throwing out statements by their clients that may have incriminated them? Although that may be a popular impression, a study by the National Institute of Justice finds otherwise.[20] This survey compared arrests in Jacksonville, Florida, with those in San Diego, California. There were nearly twice as many suspects in San Diego as in Jacksonville who decided to "remain silent." Yet that made hardly any difference to the outcomes in court. Only about one percent of those arrested asked later that their statements be suppressed. Only half of those (3 out of 619) requests were granted. Only one was granted due to "failure to give *Miranda* warnings."[21]

The Rights of Teenagers

So far, it has not been clear how *Miranda* rights affect teenagers, rather than adult suspects. Since the late nineteenth century, teen offenses have been heard in a system of juvenile courts. This system was meant to keep children from being handled like adults in courts and prisons. Yet in a 1967 Arizona case, *In re Gault*, the Supreme Court found that the juvenile courts sacrificed constitutional rights for informality.[22]

Fifteen-year-old Gerald Gault was arrested after a neighbor complained that he had made obscene phone calls to her. Gerald was convicted in juvenile court of being a delinquent. He was sentenced to six years in a state industrial school. He was never given the right to remain silent or to ask for an attorney. He was also never given a notice of the charges against him, the right to confront the neighbor in court, or the chance to appeal his sentence.

Justice Abe Fortas spoke for the seven Justices who reversed the decision of the Arizona juvenile court that had originally convicted Gerald Gault. It was, he said, a violation of "due process." This is the standard of fairness set out in the Fourteenth Amendment before a citizen may be deprived of "life, liberty or property." Specifically, the majority said that among essential rights applying to youthful and adult offenders was "the privilege against self-incrimination" of the Fifth Amendment. The rights to an attorney, to a notice of charges, and to "sworn testimony subjected to the opportunity of cross-examination" were also violated.[23]

The *Gault* decision made sure that the police will read the *Miranda* warning to juveniles before they question them. Besides the right to remain silent, youthful suspects were in 1970 guaranteed that they can be convicted of crimes only under the same standard of guilt that applies to adults.[24] They must be proved guilty beyond a reasonable doubt. They also were given another Fifth Amendment right, protection against double jeopardy, in a 1975 decision.[25] Juvenile courts offer special rights to defendants, such as keeping their names confidential. But they also give them their basic constitutional rights. These include those found in the Bill of Rights.

The Takings Clause

The right to remain silent continues to be the most controversial section of the Fifth Amendment. The right to "just compensation" (under the so-called Takings Clause) has also led to recent debates in the courts and the media. Sometimes cases still concern the model situation where someone's home is in the way of a state highway. The homeowner generally has to yield for the common good as defined by the government.

The latest cases, however, offer more complicated problems. They deal with society's attempt to save the environment. A rare species—for example, the spotted owl—may be threatened by extensive lumber operations in the Northwest. The taking here is not as obvious as in the case of a private homeowner. The ban on further timber cutting affects the property rights of the company that owns the trees. It may also cost the jobs of lumbermen who are laid off. Should judges allow a government agency to protect the environment or should they side with the lumber company and its employees? It might seem at first that the courts should side with the workers. If a forest is cut down, however, future generations would not be able to enjoy visiting it. Animals would also lose their habitats. Without trees, the land would be exposed to erosion and flooding. Letting the owners of forests cut them down at will would seem to go against the good of the community in the long run.

These complicated questions arose in the 1994 case of *Dolan* v. *City of Tigard*.[26] Mrs. Dolan objected to a city land-use plan. The plan set aside 15 percent of new business construction as open space. She wanted to double the size of her plumbing and electrical supplies store, without accepting the city's conditions. Tigard city officials claimed the regulations were necessary to avoid traffic jams and the flooding of nearby Fenno Creek.

Chief Justice Rehnquist's opinion said that such regulations were in the same class as other takings. The lower courts had been wrong to assume that the city's conditions were automatically justified. Instead, they should balance Mrs. Dolan's and the city's interests, to achieve rough proportionality. A new trial would have to be held, accounting for all these considerations. One commentator called the decision "a step in the right direction," finding it an overdue move to consider a property owner's burdens.[27] Justice Stevens was one of the four dissenters in the case. He thought Mrs. Dolan had already been offered something by the city for giving up part of her property rights. The open land would help her and other property owners by increasing drainage. Stevens also said that the city's purpose of reducing auto traffic was reasonable and, indeed, amounted to giving her just compensation.

The Fifth Amendment in Action

People have come to view the Fifth Amendment as providing essential safeguards against powers of the national government. Since the Supreme Court incorporated its key provisions—that is, made them apply to powers of the states as well—this amendment has assured Americans of fair treatment when they are suspects in a criminal case or face seizure of their property in the face of eminent domain. The courts continue to extend the reach of the people's basic rights to new circumstances.

The Founding Fathers could not imagine today's technical threats to individual freedom, such as electronic eavesdropping. They did not share our concerns with threats to endangered species or other aspects of the environment. It is one of the unique features of our system of constitutional law. Basic principles—particularly those setting limits to governmental power—can be applied to new conditions by building on precedents, or prior decisions in the field.

In each case, there are attorneys on both sides arguing about where the limits should be set. Even the Justices of the Supreme Court disagree. Sometimes it is just a bare majority of 5 to 4 that determines the latest word in the current meaning of a clause in the Fifth Amendment. But everyone agrees essentially on the amendment's statement of every person's rights: to remain silent, to avoid double jeopardy, to due process, to just compensation, and (in some state and all federal courts) the right to indictments by a grand jury.

You can use your awareness of Fifth Amendment rights to take a critical look at news on television or in the newspaper. Do reported arrests show that suspects—even juveniles—were advised of their rights? Does your community's police force offer a way to protest the illegal use of force? Are young people on the street threatened with charges under vague offenses, such as "loitering"?

One of the most informative ways to see your basic rights in action would be to sit in on a criminal trial. Either individually, or as a class project, you might arrange a visit to the nearest courthouse. You could focus on the arguments of prosecutors and defense lawyers. Was the defendant's confession obtained after *Miranda* warnings were issued? Did the police officers gather evidence in a fair manner, using due process? How does the lawyer bring in matters that relate to the Bill of Rights, especially the Fifth Amendment?

You might also invite a lawyer to your social studies class to talk about how he or she uses arguments from constitutional law in court. Did the outcome of a particular case depend on an opinion from the Supreme Court defining basic rights?

The Fifth Amendment has a living history. It provides our communities with a means to fight crime while still protecting the rights of all citizens, including suspects. Through observations of the law in action, you can begin to see how the Fifth Amendment is indeed a part of our lives.

THE CONSTITUTION OF THE UNITED STATES

The text of the Constitution is presented here. All words are given their modern spelling and capitalization. Brackets [ ] indicate parts that have been changed or set aside by amendments.

Preamble

We the people of the United States, in order to form a more perfect Union, establish justice, insure domestic tranquility, provide for the common defense, promote the general welfare, and secure the blessings of liberty to ourselves and our posterity, do ordain and establish this Constitution for the United States of America.

ARTICLE I
The Legislative Branch

Section 1. All legislative powers herein granted shall be vested in a Congress of the United States, which shall consist of a Senate and House of Representatives.

The House of Representatives

Section 2. (1) The House of Representatives shall be composed of members chosen every second year by the people of the several states, and the electors in each state shall have the qualifications requisite for electors of the most numerous branch of the state legislature.

(2) No person shall be a representative who shall not have attained the age of twenty-five years, and been seven years a citizen of the United States, and who shall not, when elected, be an inhabitant of that state in which he shall be chosen.

(3) Representatives and direct taxes shall be apportioned among the several states which may be included within this Union, according to their respective numbers, [which shall be determined by adding to the whole number of free persons, including those bound to service for a term of years, and excluding Indians not taxed, three-fifths of all other persons]. The actual enumeration shall be made within three years after the first meeting of the Congress of the United States, and within every subsequent term of ten years, in such manner as they shall by law direct. The number of representatives shall not exceed one for every thirty thousand, but each state shall have at least one representative; [and until such enumeration shall be made, the state of New Hampshire shall be entitled to choose three, Massachusetts eight, Rhode Island and Providence Plantations one, Connecticut five, New York six, New Jersey four, Pennsylvania eight, Delaware one, Maryland six, Virginia ten, North Carolina five, South Carolina five, and Georgia three].

(4) When vacancies happen in the representation from any state, the executive authority thereof shall issue writs of election to fill such vacancies.

(5) The House of Representatives shall choose their Speaker and other officers; and shall have the sole power of impeachment.

The Senate

Section 3. (1) The Senate of the United States shall be composed of two senators from each state, [chosen by the legislature thereof,] for six years; and each senator shall have one vote.

(2) Immediately after they shall be assembled in consequence of the first election, they shall be divided as equally as may be into three classes. The seats of the senators of the first class shall be vacated at the expiration of the second year, of the second class at the expiration of the fourth year, and of the third class at the expiration of the sixth year, so that one-third may be chosen every second year; [and if vacancies happen by resignation, or otherwise, during the recess of the legislature of any state, the executive thereof may make temporary appointments until the next meeting of the legislature, which shall then fill such vacancies].

(3) No person shall be a senator who shall not have attained to the age of thirty years, and been nine years a citizen of the United States, and who shall not, when elected, be an inhabitant of that state for which he shall be chosen.

(4) The Vice President of the United States shall be president of the Senate, but shall have no vote, unless they be equally divided.

(5) The Senate shall choose their other officers, and also a president *pro tempore*, in the absence of the Vice President, or when he shall exercise the office of President of the United States.

(6) The Senate shall have the sole power to try all impeachments. When sitting for that purpose, they shall be on oath or affirmation. When the President of the United States is tried, the Chief Justice shall preside: and no person shall be convicted without the concurrence of two-thirds of the members present.

(7) Judgement in cases of impeachment shall not extend further than to removal from office, and disqualification to hold and enjoy any office of honor, trust, or profit under the United States: but the party convicted shall nevertheless be liable and subject to indictment, trial, judgement and punishment, according to law.

Organization of Congress

Section 4. (1) The times, places and manner of holding elections for senators and representatives, shall be prescribed in each state by the legislature thereof; but the Congress may at any time by law make or alter such regulations, [except as to the places of choosing senators].

(2) The Congress shall assemble at least once in every year, [and such meeting shall be on the first Monday in December], unless they shall by law appoint a different day.

Section 5. (1) Each house shall be the judge of the elections, returns and qualifications of its own members, and a majority of each shall constitute a quorum to do business; but a smaller number may adjourn from day to day, and may be authorized to compel the attendance of absent members, in such manner, and under such penalties as each house may provide.

(2) Each house may determine the rules of its proceedings, punish its members for disorderly behavior, and, with the concurrence of two-thirds, expel a member.

(3) Each house shall keep a journal of its proceedings, and from time to time publish the same, excepting such parts as may in their judgement require secrecy; and the yeas and nays of the members of either house on any question shall, at the desire of one-fifth of those present, be entered on the journal.

(4) Neither house, during the session of Congress, shall, without the consent of the other, adjourn for more than three days, nor to any other place than that in which the two houses shall be sitting.

Section 6. (1) The senators and representatives shall receive a compensation for their services, to be ascertained by law, and paid out of the treasury of the United States. They shall in all cases, except treason, felony and breach of the peace, be privileged from arrest during their attendance at the session of their respective houses, and in going to and returning from the same; and for any speech or debate in either house, they shall not be questioned in any other place.

(2) No senator or representative shall, during the time for which he was elected, be appointed to any civil office under the authority of the United States, which shall have been created, or the emoluments whereof shall have been increased during such time; and no person holding any office under the United States shall be a member of either house during his continuance in office.

Section 7. (1) All bills for raising revenue shall originate in the House of Representatives; but the Senate may propose or concur with amendments as on other bills.

(2) Every bill which shall have passed the House of Representatives and the Senate, shall, before it become a law, be presented to the President of the United States; if he approve he shall sign it, but if not he shall return it, with his objections to that house in which it shall have originated, who shall enter the objections at large on their journal, and proceed to reconsider it. If after such reconsideration two-thirds of that house shall agree to pass the bill, it shall be sent, together with the objections, to the other house, by which it shall likewise be reconsidered, and if approved by two-thirds of that house, it shall become a law. But in all such cases the votes of both houses shall be determined by yeas and nays, and the names of the persons voting for and against the bill shall be entered on the journal of each house respectively. If any bill shall not be returned by the President within ten days (Sundays excepted) after it shall have been presented to him, the same shall be a law, in like manner as if he had signed it, unless the Congress by their

adjournment prevent its return, in which case it shall not be a law.

(3) Every order, resolution, or vote to which the concurrence of the Senate and House of Representatives may be necessary (except on a question of adjournment) shall be presented to the President of the United States; and before the same shall take effect, shall be approved by him, or being disapproved by him, shall be repassed by two-thirds of the Senate and House of Representatives, according to the rules and limitations prescribed in the case of a bill.

Powers Granted to Congress

The Congress shall have power:

Section 8. (1) To lay and collect taxes, duties, imposts and excises, to pay the debts and provide for the common defense and general welfare of the United States; but all duties, imposts and excises shall be uniform throughout the United States;

(2) To borrow money on the credit of the United States;

(3) To regulate commerce with foreign nations, and among the several states, and with the Indian tribes;

(4) To establish an uniform rule of naturalization, and uniform laws on the subject of bankruptcies throughout the United States;

(5) To coin money, regulate the value thereof, and of foreign coin, and fix the standard of weights and measures;

(6) To provide for the punishment of counterfeiting the securities and current coin of the United States;

(7) To establish post offices and post roads;

(8) To promote the progress of science and useful arts, by securing for limited times to authors and inventors the exclusive right to their respective writings and discoveries;

(9) To constitute tribunals inferior to the Supreme Court;

(10) To define and punish piracies and felonies committed on the high seas, and offenses against the law of nations;

(11) To declare war, grant letters of marque and reprisal, and make rules concerning captures on land and water;

(12) To raise and support armies, but no appropriation of money to that use shall be for a longer term than two years;

(13) To provide and maintain a navy;

(14) To make rules for the government and regulation of the land and naval forces;

(15) To provide for calling forth the militia to execute the laws of the Union, suppress insurrections and repel invasions;

(16) To provide for organizing, arming, and disciplining the militia, and for governing such part of them as may be employed in the service of the United States, reserving to the states respectively, the appointment of the officers, and the authority of training the militia according to the discipline prescribed by Congress;

(17) To exercise exclusive legislation in all cases whatsoever, over such district (not exceeding ten miles square) as may, by cession of particular states, and the acceptance of Congress, become the seat of the government of the United States, and to exercise like authority over all places purchased by the consent of the legislature of the state in which the same shall be, for the erection of forts, magazines, arsenals, dockyards, and other needful buildings;—And

(18) To make all laws which shall be necessary and proper for carrying into execution the foregoing powers, and all other powers vested by this Constitution in the government of the United States, or in any department or officer thereof.

Powers Forbidden to Congress

Section 9. (1) The migration or importation of such persons as any of the states now existing shall think proper to admit, shall not be prohibited by the Congress prior to the year one thousand eight hundred and eight, but a tax or duty may be imposed on such importation, not exceeding ten dollars for each person.

(2) The privilege of the writ of *habeas corpus* shall not be suspended, unless when in cases of rebellion or invasion the public safety may require it.

(3) No bill of attainder or *ex post facto* law shall be passed.

(4) No capitation, [or other direct,] tax shall be laid, unless in proportion to the census or enumeration herein before directed to be taken.

(5) No tax or duty shall be laid on articles exported from any state.

(6) No preference shall be given by any regulation of commerce or revenue to the ports of one state over those of another: nor shall vessels bound to, or from, one state, be obliged to enter, clear, or pay duties in another.

(7) No money shall be drawn from the treasury, but in consequence of appropriations made by law; and a regular statement and account of the receipts and expenditures of all public money shall be published from time to time.

(8) No title of nobility shall be granted by the United States: And no person holding any office or profit or trust under them, shall, without the consent of the Congress, accept of any present, emolument, office, or title, of any kind whatsoever, from any king, prince, or foreign state.

Powers Forbidden to the States

Section 10. (1) No state shall enter into any treaty, alliance, or confederation; grant letters of marque and reprisal; coin money; emit bills of credit; make any thing but gold and silver coin a tender in payment of debts; pass any bill of attainder, *ex post facto* law, or law impairing the obligation of contracts, or grant any title of nobility.

(2) No state shall, without the consent of the Congress, lay any imposts or duties on imports or exports, except what may be absolutely necessary for executing its inspection laws: and the net produce of all duties and imposts, laid by any state on imports or exports, shall be for the use of the treasury of the United States, and all such laws shall be subject to the revision and control of the Congress.

(3) No state shall, without the consent of Congress, lay any duty of tonnage, keep troops, or ships of war in time of peace, enter into any agreement or compact with another state, or with a foreign power, or engage in war, unless actually invaded, or in such imminent danger as will not admit of delay.

Article II
The Executive Branch

Section 1. (1) The executive power shall be vested in a President of the United States of America. He shall hold his office during the term of four years, and, together with the Vice President, chosen for the same term, be elected as follows:

(2) Each state shall appoint, in such manner as the legislature thereof may direct, a number of electors, equal to the whole number of senators and representatives to which the state may be entitled in the Congress: but no senator or representative, or person holding an office of trust or profit under the United States, shall be appointed an elector.

(3) [The electors shall meet in their respective states, and vote by ballot for two persons, of whom one at least shall not be an inhabitant of the same state with themselves. And they shall make a list of all the persons voted for, and of the number of votes for each; which list they shall sign and certify, and transmit sealed to the seat of government of the United States, directed to the president of the Senate. The president of the Senate shall, in the presence of the Senate and House of Representatives, open all the certificates, and the votes shall then be counted. The person having the greatest number of votes shall be the President, if such number be a majority of the whole number of electors appointed; and if there be more than one who have such majority, and have an equal number of votes, then the House of Representatives shall immediately choose by ballot one of them for President; and if no person have a majority, then from the five highest on the list the said House shall in like manner choose the President. But in choosing the President, the votes shall be taken by states, the representation from each state having one vote; a quorum for this purpose shall consist of a member or members from two-thirds of the states, and a majority of all the states shall be necessary to a choice. In every case, after the choice of the President, the person having the greatest number of votes of the electors shall be the Vice President. But if there should remain two or more who have equal votes, the Senate shall choose from them by ballot the Vice President.]

(4) The Congress may determine the time of choosing the electors, and the day on which they shall give their

votes; which day shall be the same throughout the United States.

(5) No person except a natural-born citizen, or a citizen of the United States, at the time of the adoption of this Constitution, shall be eligible to the office of President; neither shall any person be eligible to that office who shall not have attained to the age of thirty-five years, and been fourteen years a resident within the United States.

(6) In case of the removal of the President from office, or of his death, resignation, or inability to discharge the powers and duties of the said office, the same shall devolve on the Vice President, and the Congress may by law provide for the case of removal, death, resignation, or inability, both of the President and Vice President, declaring what officer shall then act as President, and such officer shall act accordingly, until the disability be removed, or a President shall be elected.

(7) The President shall, at stated times, receive for his services, a compensation, which shall neither be increased nor diminished during the period for which he shall have been elected, and he shall not receive within that period any other emolument from the United States, or any of them.

(8) Before he enter on the execution of his office, he shall take the following oath or affirmation: "I do solemnly swear (or affirm) that I will faithfully execute the office of the President of the United States, and will to the best of my ability, preserve, protect and defend the Constitution of the United States."

Section 2. (1) The President shall be commander-in-chief of the Army and Navy of the United States, and of the militia of the several states, when called into the actual service of the United States; he may require the opinion, in writing, of the principal officer in each of the executive departments, upon any subject relating to the duties of their respective offices, and he shall have power to grant reprieves and pardons for offenses against the United States, except in cases of impeachment.

(2) He shall have power, by and with the advice and consent of the Senate, to make treaties, provided two-thirds of the senators present concur; and he shall nominate, and by and with the advice and consent of the Senate, shall appoint ambassadors, other public ministers and consuls, judges of the Supreme Court, and all other officers of the United States, whose appointments are not herein otherwise provided for, and which shall be established by law: but the Congress may by law vest the appointment of such inferior officers, as they think proper, in the President alone, in the courts of law, or in the heads of departments.

(3) The President shall have the power to fill up all vacancies that may happen during the recess of the Senate, by granting commissions which shall expire at the end of their next session.

Section 3. He shall from time to time give to the Congress information of the state of the Union, and recommend to their consideration such measures as he shall judge necessary and expedient; he may, on extraordinary occasions, convene both houses, or either of them, and in case of disagreement between them, with respect to the time of adjournment, he may adjourn them to such time as he shall think proper; he shall receive ambassadors and other public ministers; he shall take care that the laws be faithfully executed, and shall commission all the officers of the United States.

Section 4. The President, Vice President and all civil officers of the United States, shall be removed from office on impeachment for, and conviction of, treason, bribery, or other high crimes and misdemeanors.

ARTICLE III
The Judicial Branch

Section 1. The judicial power of the United States, shall be vested in one Supreme Court, and in such inferior courts as the Congress may from time to time ordain and establish. The judges, both of the Supreme and inferior courts, shall hold their offices during good behaviour, and shall, at stated times, receive for their services, a compensation, which shall not be diminished during their continuance in office.

Section 2. (1) The judicial power shall extend to all cases, in law and equity, arising under this Constitution, the laws of the United States, and treaties made, or which shall be made, under their authority; —to all cases affecting ambassadors, other public ministers and consuls;—to all cases of admiralty and maritime jurisdiction;—to controversies to which the United States shall be a party;—to controversies between two or more states, [between a state and citizens of another state;], between citizens of different states;—between citizens of the same state claiming lands under grants of different states, and between a state, or the citizens thereof, and foreign states, [citizens or subjects].

(2) In all cases affecting ambassadors, other public ministers and consuls, and those in which a state shall be party, the Supreme Court shall have original jurisdiction. In all the other cases before mentioned, the Supreme Court shall have appellate jurisdiction, both as to law and fact, with such exceptions, and under such regulations as the Congress shall make.

(3) The trial of all crimes, except in cases of impeachment, shall be by jury; and such trial shall be held in the state where the said crimes shall have been committed; but when not committed within any state, the trial shall be at such place or places as the Congress may by law have directed.

Section 3. (1) Treason against the United States, shall consist only in levying war against them, or in adhering to their enemies, giving them aid and comfort. No person shall be convicted of treason unless on the testimony of two witnesses to the same overt act, or on confession in open court.

(2) The Congress shall have power to declare the punishment of treason, but no attainder of treason shall work corruption of blood, or forfeiture, except during the life of the person attainted.

ARTICLE IV
Relation of the States to Each Other
Section 1. Full faith and credit shall be given in each state to the public acts, records, and judicial

proceedings of every other state. And the Congress may by general laws prescribe the manner in which such acts, records and proceedings shall be proved, and the effect thereof.

Section 2. (1) The citizens of each state shall be entitled to all privileges and immunities of citizens in the several states.

(2) A person charged in any state with treason, felony, or other crime, who shall flee justice, and be found in another state, shall on demand of the executive authority of the state from which he fled, be delivered up, to be removed to the state having jurisdiction of the crime.

(3) [No person held to service or labor in one state, under the laws thereof, escaping into another, shall, in consequence of any law or regulation therein, be discharged from such service or labor, but shall be delivered up on claim of the party to whom such service or labor may be due.]

Federal-State Relations

Section 3. (1) New states may be admitted by the Congress into this Union; but no new state shall be formed or erected within the jurisdiction of any other state, nor any state be formed by the junction of two or more states, without the consent of the legislatures of the states concerned as well as of the Congress.

(2) The Congress shall have power to dispose of and make all needful rules and regulations respecting the territory or other property belonging to the United States; and nothing in this Constitution shall be so

construed as to prejudice any claims of the United States, or of any particular state.

Section 4. The United States shall guarantee to every state in this Union a republican form of government, and shall protect each of them against invasion; and on application of the legislature, or of the executive (when the legislature cannot be convened), against domestic violence.

ARTICLE V
Amending the Constitution

The Congress, whenever two-thirds of both houses shall deem it necessary, shall propose amendments to this Constitution, or, on the application of the legislatures of two-thirds of the several states, shall call a convention for proposing amendments, which, in either case, shall be valid to all intents and purposes, as part of this Constitution, when ratified by the legislatures of three-fourths of the several states, or by conventions in three-fourths thereof, as the one or the other mode of ratification may be proposed by the Congress; provided [that no amendment which may be made prior to the year one thousand eight hundred and eight, shall in any manner affect the first and fourth clauses in the ninth section of the first article; and] that no state, without its consent, shall be deprived of its equal suffrage in the Senate.

ARTICLE VI
National Debts

(1) All debts contracted and engagements entered into, before the adoption of this Constitution, shall be as

valid against the United States under this Constitution, as under the Confederation.

Supremacy of the National Government

(2) This Constitution, and the laws of the United States which shall be made in pursuance thereof; and all treaties made, or which shall be made, under the authority of the United States shall be the supreme law of the land; and the judges in every state shall be bound thereby, any thing in the constitution or laws of any state to the contrary notwithstanding.

(3) The senators and representatives before mentioned, and the members of the several state legislatures, and all executive and judicial officers, both of the United States and of the several states, shall be bound by oath or affirmation, to support this Constitution; but no religious test shall ever be required as a qualification to any office or public trust under the United States.

ARTICLE VII
Ratifying the Constitution

The ratification of the conventions of nine states, shall be sufficient for the establishment of this Constitution between the states so ratifying the same.

Done in convention by the unanimous consent of the states present the seventeenth day of September in the year of our Lord one thousand seven hundred and eighty-seven and of the independence of the United States of America the twelfth. In witness whereof we have hereunto subscribed our names.

Amendments to the Constitution

The first ten amendments, known as the Bill of Rights, were proposed on September 25, 1789. They were ratified, or accepted, on December 15, 1791. They were adopted because some states refused to approve the Constitution unless a Bill of Rights, protecting individuals from various unjust acts of government, was added.

Amendment 1

Freedom of religion, speech, and the press; rights of assembly and petition

Amendment 2

Right to bear arms

Amendment 3

Housing of soldiers

Amendment 4

Search and arrest warrants

Amendment 5

Rights in criminal cases

Amendment 6

Rights to a fair trial

Amendment 7

Rights in civil cases

Amendment 8

Bails, fines, and punishments

Amendment 9

Rights retained by the people

Amendment 10

Powers retained by the states and the people

Amendment 11

Lawsuits against states

Amendment 12

Election of the President and Vice President

Amendment 13

Abolition of slavery

Amendment 14

Civil rights

Amendment 15

African-American suffrage

Amendment 16

Income taxes

Amendment 17

Direct election of senators

Amendment 18

Prohibition of liquor

Amendment 19

Women's suffrage

Amendment 20

Terms of the President and Congress

Amendment 21

Repeal of prohibition

Amendment 22

Presidential term limits

Amendment 23
Suffrage in the District of Columbia

Amendment 24
Poll taxes

Amendment 25
Presidential disability and succession

Amendment 26
Suffrage for eighteen-year-olds

Amendment 27
Congressional salaries

Chapter Notes

Introduction

No Notes.

Chapter 1. Your Rights Under the Fifth Amendment

1. 384 U.S. 436 (1966).
2. Quentin Reynolds, *Courtroom: The Story of Samuel S. Leibowitz* (New York: Farrar, Straus, 1950), pp. 410–411.
3. Yale Kamisar, "*Miranda v. Arizona*," in Kermit L. Hall, ed., *The Oxford Companion to the Supreme Court of the United States* (New York: Oxford University Press, 1992), p. 553.
4. 395 U.S. 784 (1969).
5. *Schenck v. United States*, 249 U.S. 47 (1919).
6. 260 U.S. 377 (1922).
7. Lee Epstein and Thomas G. Walker, *Constitutional Law for a Changing America: Rights, Liberties, and Justice* (Washington, D.C.: Congressional Quarterly Press, 1992), pp. 333–334.
8. Ellen Alderman and Caroline Kennedy, *In Our Defense: The Bill of Rights in Action* (New York: Avon, 1992), p. 152.
9. 110 U.S. 516 (1884).
10. 291 U.S. 502 (1934).
11. 381 U.S. 479 (1965).
12. *Katz v. United States*, 389 U.S. 347 (1967).
13. 410 U.S. 113 (1973).
14. *Cruzan v. Missouri Department of Health*, 497 U.S. 336 (1990).
15. *Barron v. Baltimore*, 32 U.S. 243 (1833).
16. 166 U.S. 226 (1897).

Chapter 2. Ancestry of the Fifth Amendment

1. Bernard Schwartz, *The Great Rights of Mankind: A History of the American Bill of Rights* (Madison, Wis.: Madison House, 1992), p. 26.
2. Ibid., p. 6.
3. Ibid., pp. 9–12.
4. Ibid., p. 23.
5 Leonard W. Levy, *Origins of the Fifth Amendment: The Right Against Self-Incrimination* (New York: Oxford University Press, 1968), p. 405.
6. Ibid., p. 407.
7. Leroy D. Clark, *The Grand Jury: The Use and Abuse of Political Power* (New York: Quadrangle Press, 1975), p. 8.
8. Ibid.; Levy, p. 45.
9. Clark, p. 9.
10. Peter W. Sperlich, "Grand Juries," in Kermit Hall, ed., *The Oxford Companion to the Supreme Court of the United States* (New York: Oxford University Press, 1992), p. 344.

11. Ellen Alderman and Caroline Kennedy, *In Our Defense: The Bill of Rights in Action* (New York: Avon Books, 1992), p. 170.

12. Ibid.

13. Ibid., p. 171.

14. Levy, p. 277.

15. Ibid., p. 179.

16. Samuel Gardiner, *The Constitutional Documents of the Puritan Revolution, 1625–1660* (New York: Oxford Press, 1906), p. 179.

17. Ibid., p. 171.

18. Levy, p. 363.

19. Ibid., p. 360.

20. Ibid.

21. Alderman and Kennedy, p. 153.

Chapter 3. How the Fifth Amendment Was Born

1. Richard B. Morris, *Witness at the Creation: Hamilton, Madison, Jay, and the Constitution* (New York: Holt, Reinhart and Winston, 1985), p. 94.

2. George Anastaplo, *The Amendments to the Constitution: A Commentary* (Baltimore: Johns Hopkins University Press, 1995), p. 12.

3. Ibid., pp. 295–296.

4. Ibid., p. 296.

5. Ibid., p. 295.

6. Merrill Jensen, *The Making of the American Constitution* (Princeton, N.J.: Van Nostrand Publishers, 1964), p. 35.

7. Alexander Hamilton, James Madison, John Jay, *The Federalist Papers* (New York: New American Library, 1961), p. xi.

8. Ibid., p. 84.

9. Ibid., p. 510.

10. Ibid., p. 513.

11. Ibid., p. 514.

12. Herbert J. Storing, *What the Anti-Federalists Were For* (Chicago: University of Chicago Press, 1981), pp. 66–67.

13. Cecilia M. Kenyon, ed., *The Antifederalists* (Indianapolis: Bobbs-Merrill, 1966), p. 424.

14. Ibid., p. 426.

15. "Declaration of Rights and Amendments Proposed by the Virginia Convention," in Jonathan Elliott, *The Debates in the Several States Conventions on the Adoption of the Federal Constitution as Recommended by the General Convention at Philadelphia* (Philadelphia: J. B. Lippincott, 1881), pp. 657–663.

16. Kenyon, p. 429.

17. Ibid. p. 432.

18. Ibid., pp. 432–433.

19. Morris, p. 235.

20. Kenyon, p. 373.

21. Morris, p. 247.

22. Helen E. Veit et al., eds., *Creating the Bill of Rights: The Documentary Record From the First Federal Congress* (Baltimore: Johns Hopkins University Press, 1991), p. xi.

23. Morris, p. 204.

24. Ibid.

25. Marvin Meyers, *The Mind of the Founder: Sources of the Political Thought of James Madison* (Indianapolis: Bobbs-Merrill, 1973), p. 205.

26. Veit, p. xiii.

27. Cited in William Lee Miller, *The Business of May Next: James Madison and the Founding* (Charlottesville, Va.: University Press of Virginia, 1992), p. 257.

28. Ibid., p. 261.

Chapter 4. Fathers of the Fifth Amendment

1. William Lee Miller, *The Business of May Next: James Madison and the Founding* (Charlottesville, Va.: University Press of Virginia, 1992), p. 10.

2. Jonathan Elliott, *The Debates in the Several State Conventions on the Adoption of the Federal Constitution as Recommended by the General Convention at Philadelphia* (Philadelphia: J.B. Lippincott, 1881), 5 volumes.

3. Marvin Meyers, *The Mind of the Founder* (Indianapolis: Bobbs-Merrill, 1973). p. xxxvi.

4. Ibid., p. 204.

5. Ibid., p. 205.

6. Elliott, vol. 5, p. 568.

7. Ibid., p. 566.

8. Robert Rutland, *George Mason: Reluctant Statesman* (Charlottesville, Va.: University Press of Virginia, 1961), p. 89.

9. Miller, p. 248.

10. John C. Fitzpatrick, ed., *The Writings of George Washington from the Original Manuscript Sources, 1745–1799* (Washington, D.C.: U.S. Government Printing Office, 1939), vol. 30, p. 304.

11. Ibid., pp. 341–342.

12. Hugh Blair Grigsby, *The Virginia Convention of 1776* (New York: De Capo Press, 1969), p. 161.

13. Ibid., p. 162.

14. William T. Hutchinson and William Rachals, eds., *The Papers of James Madison* (Chicago: University of Chicago Press, 1962), vol. 12, pp. 197–210.

15. Miller, p. 254.

16. Ibid., p. 259.

Chapter 5. The Battle for Ratification

1. United States Constitution, Article VII.

2. Cecilia M. Kenyon, ed., *The Antifederalists* (Indianapolis: Bobbs-Merrill, 1966), pp. lxii–lxx.

3. Stephen R. Boyd, "Antifederalists and the Acceptance of the Constitution: Pennsylvania, *1787–1792,*" *Publius*, 1979 9:2, p.125.

4. Charles A. Beard, *An Economic Interpretation of the Constitution of the United States* (New York: Macmillan, 1935), p. 251.

5. S. E. Morison, *Oxford History of the American People* (New York: Oxford University Press, 1965), p. 313.

6. "Tench Coxe to James Madison, 9/28/1787," in William T. Hutchinson and William Rachal, eds., *The Papers of James Madison* (Chicago: University of Chicago Press, 1962) vol. 10, pp. 176–178.

7. Boyd, p. 127.

8. Craig R. Smith, *To Form a More Perfect Union: The Ratification of the Constitution and the Bill of Rights, 1787–1791* (Lanham, Md.: University Press of America, 1993), pp. 40–41.

9. Boyd, pp. 128–129.

10. Kenyon, p. 36.

11. Hutchinson and Rachal, vol. 10, p. 398.

12. Charles Warren, "Elbridge Gerry, James Warren, Mercy Warren, and the Ratification of the Federal Constitution in Massachusetts," *Proceedings of the Massachusetts Historical Society*, vol. 64, pp. 148–149.

13. Smith, pp. 57–58.

14. Ibid., p. 66.

15. Morison, p. 314.

16. "Washington to Marquis de Lafayette, May 28, 1788, in John C. Fitzpatrick, *The Writings of George Washington*, vol. 29 (Washington, D.C.: U.S. Government Printing Office, 1939), pp. 507–508.

17. Philip A. Bruce, *The Virginia Plutarch* (Chapel Hill, N.C.: University of North Carolina Press, 1929), vol. 1, pp. 189–190.

18. Henry Mayer, *A Son of Thunder: Patrick Henry and the American Republic* (New York: Franklin Watts Publishers, 1986), p. 14.

19. Ibid., p. 225.

20. Ibid., p. 227.

21. Jonathan Elliott, *The Debates in Several State Conventions*, vol. 3 (Philadelphia: J. B. Lippincott, 1881), p. 652.

22. Bruce, p. 191.

23. Harold Syrett and Jacob Cooke, eds., *Papers of Alexander Hamilton*, vol. 5 (New York: Columbia University Press, 1962), p. 140.

24. Robin Brooks, "Alexander Hamilton, Melancton Smith, and the Ratification of the Constitution in New York," *William and Mary Quarterly*, vol. 24, p. 341.

25. Smith, p. 119.

26. Syrett and Cooke, eds., vol. 5, p. 184.

27. Ibid., p. 185.

28. Brooks, p. 356.

29. Smith, p. 161.

Chapter 6. The Fifth Amendment Today

1. 378 U.S. 478 (1964).

2. Ibid.

3. Yale Kamisar, "*Miranda* v. *Arizona*," in Kermit L. Hall, ed., *The Oxford Companion to the Supreme Court of the United States* (New York: Oxford University Press, 1992), p. 552.

4. Fred Graham, "High Court Puts New Curbs on Powers of Police to Interrogate Suspects," *The New York Times*, June 14, 1996, p. 1.

5. *Orozco v. Texas*, 394 U.S. 324 (1969).

6. Ibid.

7. Earl Warren, *The Memoirs of Chief Justice Earl Warren* (New York: Doubleday, 1977), p. 316.

8. Ibid.

9. *Beckwith v. United States*, 425 U.S. 341 (1976).

10. *Oregon v. Mathiason*, 429 U.S. 711 (1977).

11. *Rhode Island v. Innis*, 446 U.S. 291 (1980).

12. David O'Brien, *Constitutional Law and Politics II: Civil Rights and Civil Liberties* (New York: W. W. Norton, 1991), pp. 965–968.

13. *Colorado v. Connelly*, 479 U.S. 157 (1986).

14. *Pennsylvania v. Burder*, 489 U.S. 9 (1988).

15. Paul Nappi, "*Miranda* and the Rehnquist Court: Has the Pendulum Swung Too Far?" *Boston College Law Review*, March 1989, 30:2, pp. 523–571.

16. Ibid., p. 571.

17. Richard Leo, "The Impact of *Miranda* Revisited," *Journal of Criminal Law and Criminology*, 86:3, p. 622.

18. Ibid.

19. Ibid., p. 652.

20. Floyd Feeney et al., *Arrests Without Conviction: How Often They Occur and Why* (Washington, D.C.: U.S. Department of Justice, 1983), p. 144.

21. Ibid., p. 145.

22. 387 U.S. 1 (1967).

23. Ibid.

24. *In re Winship*, 397 U.S. 358 (1970).

25. *Breed v. Jones*, 421 U.S. 519 (1975).

26. 114 S. Ct. 2309 (1994).

27. James Huffman, "*Dolan v. City of Tigard*: Another Step in the Right Direction," *Environmental Law*, Winter 1995, 25:1, pp. 143–153.

Glossary

Anti-Federalists—Those who opposed ratifying the Constitution because they feared a strong national government. They included farmers, city workers, and debtors.

Bill of Rights—The first ten amendments added to the Constitution in 1791.

civil trial—A legal action under noncriminal law that seeks to recover damages (in the form of money).

common law—Judge-made law, which the United States adapted from England, where it was supposed to reflect the customary rules of the people.

Connecticut Compromise—The fusion of the Virginia and the New Jersey plans at the Constitutional Convention of 1787. It combined a Senate (made up of two senators per state) with a House of Representatives in which seats were allotted by population.

criminal trial—A legal action against someone accused of crimes against the state. Punishments include fines and imprisonment.

dissent—An opinion written by a Justice who disagrees with the majority of the Court.

double jeopardy—Being tried twice for the same crime. This practice is prohibited by the Fifth Amendment.

due process—Fair and regular procedure provided by law, which is guaranteed to people by the Fifth and Fourteenth Amendments to the Constitution.

eminent domain—The power of the government to take private property for public purposes.

Federalists—A political party organized in 1787 to help achieve ratification of the Constitution. It included planters, merchants, bankers, and manufacturers. They sought a strong central government.

grand jury—A group of twelve to twenty-three persons that hears, in private, evidence for serving an indictment.

habeas corpus—Literally, "you have the body." It is a writ issued to a person under arrest to grant freedom unless the government can demonstrate sufficient evidence to justify holding him or her for trial.

immunity—A grant of exemption from prosecution in return for a person's testimony. If the person accepts, he or she gives up the right against self-incrimination.

incorporation doctrine—The theory adopted by the Supreme Court since the mid-1930s that applies key parts of the Bill of Rights to the states and the federal government.

Magna Carta—The "Great Charter" granted by King John of England to the barons at Runnymeade in 1215. It proclaims basic rights under English law.

***Miranda* warning**—The caution that police must give criminal suspects in custody, in accord with the Supreme Court's 1966 decision. It warns suspects that they have a right to remain silent, that anything they say can and will be held against them in a court of law, and that they have a right to an attorney.

New Jersey Plan—The proposal submitted by William Patterson to the Constitutional Convention. It reflected the wishes of small states for equal representation in Congress.

opinion—A written explanation of a judge's decision. It discusses the legal precedents and the reasoning of the court.

precedents—Prior legal decisions about an issue currently before a court. The court is expected to decide a case in a way that is consistent with precedent.

Reconstruction—The period of time after the Civil War that reflected an effort to bring back into the Union the states that had seceded. It also refers to federal efforts to rebuild these states economically and politically.

self-incrimination—Providing testimony or evidence against oneself in a criminal trial or investigation. The Fifth Amendment protects a suspect or witness from being forced to testify against himself or herself.

Takings Clause—A section of the Fifth Amendment that states that private property may be taken by the government for public use if fair compensation is provided in exchange.

Virginia Plan—The proposal offered by Edmund Randolph at the Constitutional Convention in 1787. It proposed basing representation in Congress on population. This plan was favored by the more populated states.

Further Reading

Alderman, Ellen, and Caroline Kennedy. *In Our Defense: The Bill of Rights in Action*. New York: Avon, 1992.

Feldman, Daniel L. *The Logic of American Government: Applying the Constitution to the Contemporary World*. New York: William Morrow, 1990.

Friendly, Fred W., and Martha J. H. Elliott. *The Constitution: That Delicate Balance*. New York: Random House, 1984.

Garraty, John A. *Quarrels That Have Shaped the Constitution*. New York: Harper & Row, 1987.

Hall, Kermit L. *The Oxford Companion to the Supreme Court of the United States*. New York: Oxford University Press, 1992.

Herda, D.J. *Earl Warren: Chief Justice for Social Change*. Springfield, N.J.: Enslow Publishers, Inc., 1995.

Judson, Karen. *The Constitution of the United States*. Springfield, N.J.: Enslow Publishers, Inc., 1996.

Kronenwetter, Michael, *The Supreme Court of the United States*. Springfield, N.J.: Enslow Publishers, Inc., 1996.

Internet Sites

http://caselaw.lp.findlaw.com/data/constitution/amendment05/

http://gi.grolier.com/presidents/aae/side/05amend.html

http://oyez.nwu.edu/

Index